MICHAEL

MICHAEL

BY THE EDITORS OF ROLLING STONE

HarperStudio

AN IMPRINT OF HarperCollinsPublishers

Jann S. Wenner
EDITOR AND PUBLISHER

MANAGING EDITOR: *Will Dana*

EDITOR: *Jason Fine*

ART DIRECTOR: *Joseph Hutchinson*

DIRECTOR OF PHOTOGRAPHY: *Jodi Peckman*

DEPUTY MANAGING EDITOR: *John Dioso*

CONTRIBUTING EDITORS: *Nathan Brackett, Michael Endelman, Tom Nawrocki, Jonathan Ringen*

DEPUTY ART DIRECTOR: *Mac Lewis*

PHOTO EDITORS: *Deborah Dragon, Sacha Lecca*

COPY EDITORS: *Julia Holmes, Sarene Leeds, Brian Moran, Jamie Reynolds*

RESEARCHERS: *Erika Berlin, Bob Hammond, Eric Magnuson, Kevin O'Donnell, Phoebe St. John, Alexis Sottile*

PRODUCTION MANAGER: *Eleni Tzinakos*

MICHAEL. Copyright © 2009 by Rolling Stone LLC. All rights reserved. Printed in the United States of America. No part of this book may be used or reproduced in any manner whatsoever without written permission except in the case of brief quotations embodied in critical articles and reviews. For information address HarperCollins Publishers, 10 East 53rd Street, New York, NY 10022.

HarperCollins books may be purchased for educational, business, or sales promotional use. For information please write: Special Markets Department, HarperCollins Publishers, 10 East 53rd Street, New York, NY 10022.

For more information about this book or other books from HarperStudio, visit www.theharperstudio.com.

FIRST EDITION

Library of Congress Cataloging-in-Publication Data has been applied for.

ISBN 978-0-06-196983-6

09 10 11 12 13   QWV   10 9 8 7 6 5 4 3 2 1

CONTENTS

THE LAST EMPEROR

By Will.i.am

I WAS RAISED IN THE PROJECTS. WHEN YOU GROW up around violence and people selling crack, going to prison and dying, the only thing you have for escape is music. When you're listening to music because there's a lot of drama surrounding you, it's like a spaceship that launches you to a whole different place. That's what Michael Jackson was for me.

But why do we all love Michael Jackson? Why is Michael Jackson important? Because of his supreme talent. His ability to master his body – his vocals, his dancing. And because of his imagination, his ability to think, not even outside the box, but to think until the box doesn't exist anymore.

Michael did it the best, and I'm not just talking about performance and sales. He did it on a business level, on the level of entrepreneurship. In that sense, he was not just the King of Pop but the King of the Industry. He was like the Wall Street of music. There would be no Jay-Z if it wasn't for Michael Jackson. There would be no Usher or Justin Timberlake. All those people go away if you take Michael Jackson out of the equation.

I worked with him on the 25th-anniversary reissue of *Thriller* and on the album he was working on when he died. Initially, being in the studio with him was hard because you can't help but be a fan. I asked all the questions I always wanted to ask: "What was it like when you did the 'Thriller' video?" "Why the glitter socks?"

I told him that when he did the "Thriller" video, it was right down the street from my house. I asked my mother if I could go, but she told me no. "But why?" he asked. I explained that it was because we lived in a bad neighborhood, and it might be dangerous. He just said, "Well, then, if she had told you yes, we might not be here right now." We created a real bond. We became friends.

For the new album, he would always say that he wanted the record to be "unprecedented." I had never used that word, so I went home and looked it up. We need to go for the throat, he said. Number one. We need to be number one everywhere. He wanted to outdo himself. I would tell him that he couldn't outdo what he did. We had real conversations like that, and we did some great stuff. I hope it comes out.

When I worked with him, he was top-notch vocally and spiritually. Going through life with constant scrutiny and criticism – I don't know how he did it. Being judged and questioned by the whole world. He was still excited about music, still excited to go to rehearsals and work with people around the globe.

To understand Michael Jackson, you've got to realize where he comes from. In 2005, around the time I was working with him, I had the pleasure of working with James Brown, one of Michael's idols. I told Michael that when I asked James to take a picture with me, he clapped his hands two times, and some lady jumped out of the corner and started combing his hair.

Michael just said, "Wow. Isn't show business amazing?" When he said that, everything made sense. In show business, the stage is everywhere. The stage isn't just at the Grammys. The stage is when you leave the parking lot. It's when you go to the mall. It's about inspiring, about trying your best to be perfect.

That's the reason why Michael Jackson was like royalty. When he walked down the street, it was an event. For all the people he grew up admiring, Frank Sinatra, Sammy Davis Jr., Elizabeth Taylor, the show was everywhere. Michael is the last emperor of that era.

REMEMBERING MICHAEL

MICHAEL JACKSON INVENTED MODERN pop as we know it. As the boy-child singer of the Jackson 5, he already had that voice, soaring over the fast songs ("I Want You Back," "The Love You Save") and piercing in the ballads ("I'll Be There," "Got to Be There"). If he'd never done anything beyond this – if he'd settled into the respectable career groove of a Gladys Knight or a Steve Miller – he still would be mourned and remembered today, as these songs have never left the radio.

But in August 1979, barely out of his teens, he ascended to a whole new level of megastardom with *Off the Wall*, expanding funk, Motown, rock excess and Hollywood glitz into a new sound. It was an unabashed disco record, with an anthem called "Burn This Disco Out" at a time when "disco" was the most polarizing word in music.

But it was a record that imagined the entirety of pop in disco terms, and it sounded universal on a level nobody had imagined possible before – even Donna Summer's *Bad Girls*, which had dominated 1979 radio, sounded a bit narrow in comparison. *Off the Wall* had more hits than the radio had time to play: When "Rock With You" crashed the airwaves, it was time for "Don't Stop 'Til You Get Enough" to go home, but the radio just kept right on playing it – because nobody had gotten enough. Even on his hottest dance workouts, his voice had that sad, lonely, vulnerable twitch, just as his songs felt haunted by something otherworldly and beautiful. He was as personal and eccentric as any crackpot singer-songwriter could be – yet he was also the most famous guy in the world.

The only reason *Off the Wall* isn't remembered as the greatest pop record ever is that *Thriller* was even bigger and even better. People love to argue *Off the Wall* vs. *Thriller*, but there will never be any loser in that fight. Everybody who heard *Thriller* wanted a piece of it, and every pop musician out there spent the next few years trying to catch up with it – even Michael himself. The obvious plan was for "Beat It" to crack rock radio, but rock radio had already cracked and played the hell out of "Billie Jean." And then came "Human Nature." And "P.Y.T. (Pretty Young Thing)" and "Somebody's Watching Me" and "State of Shock" and "Farewell My Summer Love." Every station on the dial seemed to thrive on his beat, as if MJ had successfully syncopated the whole world to his own breathy, intimate, insistent rhythmic tics.

Even then, anyone could hear how weird and wounded he was, yet there was something heroic in the way he turned his psychosexual agonies into such intensely emotional, impossibly exuberant music. Whether you were a metal kid, a disco kid or a New Wave synth-pop kid, *Thriller* had what you wanted. It was Number One for 22 weeks in 1983 but felt even bigger in 1984. It also created the sound of the Eighties, as the air became full of brilliant records trying to duplicate the power of "Billie Jean": Madonna's "Like a Virgin," Cyndi Lauper's "Girls Just Want to Have Fun," John Waite's "Missing You," Van Halen's "Jump," Bruce Springsteen's "Dancing in the Dark." Michael's moment was a time when the most exciting, adventurous music anywhere in the world seemed to be right there on Top 40 radio. He was the most famous, pampered star in the world, yet you rooted for him, because he came on like an underdog, a sweet, troubled kid oppressed by extraordinary gifts, renouncing the privileges of machismo, a shy boy dreaming of the street. As he memorably said in the "Thriller" video, "I'm not like other guys."

That was putting it mildly, and you could hear it in the whoops and hiccups and glides of his voice. Every aspect of his music seemed to flow out of his effervescent dance moves, as if the same spirits that drove his feet to spin and hop through his dance routines were guiding his voice. The physical grace of his stage and screen presence seemed to give him a little temporary refuge from the pain in his songs, yet he still sounded fragile and tormented, as if he'd float away.

He ended up not floating away – as he got older, his music got heavy and ordinary, and his voice lost that wiggle and bounce. By the time he started calling himself the King of Pop in 1991, it was a kingdom that didn't exist anymore, and he seemed like the only one who didn't realize it. His life, once so full of promise, became a sad parable about getting what you want, and he kept giving his fans reasons to feel burned and betrayed. Yet no matter how depressing his celebrity spectacle got, those records remained full of life. Of the many weird things about MJ, the weirdest will always be the music – tragic wages-of-fame stories and celebrity disasters are a dime a dozen, but there has never been anyone who wrote or sang like this man. Given the circumstances of his childhood, it's no surprise Michael Jackson was tortured; the surprise is that he was able to turn his torture into music that made the whole world dance.   —The Editors

THE
ROLLING ST

RS 81 APRIL 29, 1971

Rolling Stone went on the road with the Jackson 5 and a very young Michael: "I'd like to talk to you all tonight about the blues. . . . Don't nobody have the blues like I do," Michael tells the audience in Columbus, Ohio. "I may be young, but I know what it's all about."

ONE COVERS

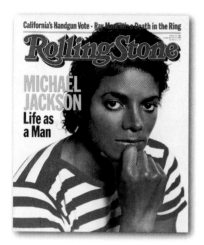

RS 389 FEBRUARY 17, 1983

A shy Jackson gives Gerri Hirshey the most-revealing print interview of his career, asking her to hold his pet snake. "I'm much more relaxed onstage than I am now," he says.

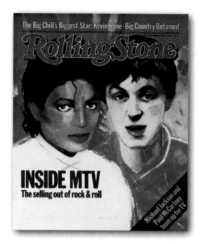

RS 410 DECEMBER 8, 1983

RS reports how Jackson helped break MTV's color line: "When 'Billie Jean' went into heavy rotation, suddenly MTV was more reflective of blacks making music too."

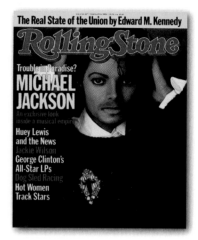

RS 417 MARCH 15, 1984

The year after the success of "Thriller," RS previews the Jacksons' "Victory" tour: "This will be one last hurrah for the Jacksons, one last blaze of cash and glory."

RS 509 SEPTEMBER 24, 1987

As he prepares to release "Bad," RS journeys inside Jackson's increasingly weird world: "His own manager describes him as a cross between E.T. and Howard Hughes."

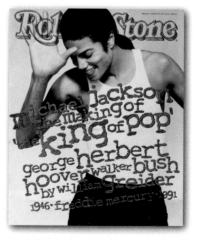

RS 621 JANUARY 9, 1992

As "Dangerous" came out, Michael opened Neverland to RS: "A narrow staircase leads to the train room. 'The kids have slumber parties up here,' says one of Jackson's staff."

RS 1084 AUGUST 6, 2009

RS investigates the final months of Michael's life: his drug addiction and intense rehearsals for what Jackson hoped would be "the greatest show on Earth."

TRIUMPH & TRAGEDY

The life of Michael Jackson
By Mikal Gilmore

THERE IS NO STORY IN POPULAR MUSIC AS PROVIDENTIAL YET AS TRAGIC AS the story of Michael Jackson. Both destinies ran throughout his life, more or less from the beginning: While still a child, he became the central source of support for a large family and an incalculable asset to one of the most important record labels in history. Jackson benefited from all of that – he won fame and money, and developed a self-image that set him apart from almost everybody. He lived vast lives within himself – it's where he brooded and transformed his resentments and desires into both blissful and fierce art. It's also where he found his strengths, and where he kept his frailties until they became lethal foibles. ★ Given his upbringing, you can see why he had to make that life within. Michael's father, Joe Jackson, was a crane operator during the 1950s, in Gary, Indiana – a place in which, according to Dave Marsh's *Trapped: Michael Jackson and the Crossover Dream,* quotas were imposed on how many black workers were allowed to advance into

skilled trades in the city's mills. Black workers were paid less than the white workers, and also suffered much higher rates of fatal industry-related illnesses – but Joe Jackson held hopes that music would lift his life. Michael's mother, Katherine Scruse, was from Alabama but was living in East Chicago, Indiana, when she met Joe. She had grown up hearing country & western music, and although she entertained her own dreams of singing and playing music, a bout of polio had left her with a permanent limp. Joe and Katherine were a young couple, married in 1949, and began a large family immediately. Their first child, Maureen (Rebbie), was born in 1950, followed by Sigmund (Jackie) in 1951, Toriano (Tito) in 1953, Jermaine in 1954, La Toya in 1956 and Marlon in 1957. Michael was born on August 29th, 1958, and Randy was born in 1961. Janet, the last born, wouldn't arrive until 1966.

SHOWBIZ KIDS
Michael (front) and his brothers in Chicago, 1968. The Jacksons had already been performing together at black nightclubs for two years.

he did everything in his domain. Katherine, though, sometimes led her children in country-music sing-alongs, during which she taught them to harmonize. Tito, like his father, had a quick affinity for playing instruments, and one day after retrieving Joe's guitar to practice with his brothers, he broke a string. As Michael later recalled, Joe whipped Tito for the infraction – "He let him have it" – then challenged his son to show him what he could play. As it turned out, Tito impressed his father. Maybe in those moments Joe Jackson saw a future hope blossom again. He bought Tito his own guitar and taught him some Ray Charles music, then he got Jermaine a bass. Soon he was working all his sons into an ensemble. Though Joe was at heart a blues man, he appreciated that contemporary R&B – Motown and soul – was the music that attracted his sons. Joe groomed Jermaine to be

Michael and his siblings heard music all the time. Joe had a strong inclination toward the rowdy electric urban blues that had developed in nearby Chicago, and also for early rock & roll. Along with his brothers, Joe formed a band, the Falcons, and made some modest extra income from playing bars and college dances around Gary. "They would do some of the great early rock & roll and blues songs by Chuck Berry, Little Richard…you name it," Michael wrote in his 1988 autobiography, *Moonwalk.* "All those styles were amazing and each had an influence on…us, though we were too young to know it at the time." When the Falcons folded, Joe retired his guitar to a bedroom closet, and he guarded it jealously, just as

lead singer, but one day, Katherine saw Michael, just four at the time, singing along to a James Brown song, and Michael – in both his voice and moves – was already eclipsing his older brother. She told Joe, "I think we have another lead singer." Katherine would later say that sometimes Michael's precocious abilities frightened her – she probably saw that his childhood might give way to stardom – but she also recognized that there was something undeniable about his young voice, that it could communicate longings and experiences that no child could yet know. Michael was also a natural center of attention. He loved singing and dancing, and because he was so young – such an unexpected vehicle for a rousing, dead-on soulful expression

GOLDEN BOYS

*From left: Jackie, Michael, Randy (standing), Jermaine, Marlon
and Tito Jackson at their Encino, California, home in 1972. In his
teens, Michael was frustrated with the group's lack of creative
control. He was worried it would become "an oldies act."*

– he became an obvious point of attention when he and his brothers performed. Little Michael Jackson was cute, but little Michael Jackson was also dynamite.

It's clear that Joe Jackson was good at what he did. "He knew exactly what I had to do to become a professional," Michael later said. "He taught me exactly how to hold a mike and make gestures to the crowd and how to handle an audience." But by Joe's own admission he was also unrelenting. "When I found out that my kids were interested in becoming entertainers, I really went to work with them," he told *Time* in 1984. "I rehearsed them about three years before I turned them loose. That's practically every day, for at least two or three hours.... They got a little upset about the whole thing in the beginning because the other kids

were out having a good time.... Then I saw that after they became better, they enjoyed it more." That isn't always how Michael remembered it. "We'd perform for him, and he'd critique us," he wrote in *Moonwalk*. "If you messed up, you got hit, sometimes with a belt, sometimes with a switch.... I'd get beaten for things that happened mostly outside rehearsal. Dad would make me so mad and hurt that I'd try to get back at him and get beaten all the more. I'd take a shoe and throw it at him, or I'd just fight back, swinging my fists. That's why I got it more than all my brothers combined. I'd fight back, and my father would kill me, just tear me up." Those moments – and probably many more – created a loss that Jackson never got over. He was essential to the family's musicmaking, but there was no other bond between father and

23

LIVE FUNK
Tito, Marlon, Michael, Jackie and Jermaine Jackson (from left) performing on TV, circa 1971

FAMILY BUSINESS
*Above: The Jacksons in 1971. Top right: Joe Jackson, a
former Indiana millworker and amateur blues guitarist,
worked his sons into an R&B ensemble in the mid-1960s.
Far right: Michael at a concert rehearsal in L.A. in 1971.
Bottom right: Young Michael at the mike.*

son. Again, from *Moonwalk*: "One of the few things I regret most is never being able to have a real closeness with him. He built a shell around himself over the years, and once he stopped talking about our family business, he found it hard to relate to us. We'd all be together, and he'd just leave the room."

Around 1964, Joe began entering the Jackson brothers in talent contests, many of which they handily won. A single they cut for the local Steeltown recording label, "Big Boy," achieved local success. "At first I told myself they were just kids," Joe said in 1971. "I soon realized they were very professional. There was nothing to wait for. The boys were ready for stage training, and I ran out of reasons to keep them from the school of hard knocks." In 1966, he booked his sons into Gary's black nightclubs, as well as some in Chicago. Many of the clubs served alcohol, and several featured strippers. "This is quite a life for a nine-year-old," Katherine would remind her husband, but Joe was undaunted. "I used to stand in the wings of this one place in Chicago and watch a lady whose name was Mary Rose," Michael recalled. "This girl would take off her clothes and her panties and throw them to the audience. The men would pick them up and sniff them and yell. My brothers and I would be watching all this, taking it in, and my father wouldn't mind." Sam Moore, of Sam and Dave, recalled

Joe locking Michael – who was maybe 10 years old – in a dressing room while Joe went off on his own adventures. Michael sat alone for hours. He also later recalled having to go onstage even if he'd been sick in bed that day.

Michael and his brothers began to tour on what was still referred to as the "chitlin circuit" – a network of black venues throughout the U.S. (Joe made sure his sons kept their school studies up to date and maintained their grades at an acceptable level.) In these theaters and clubs, the Jacksons opened for numerous R&B artists, including the Temptations, Sam and Dave, Jackie Wilson, Jerry Butler, the O'Jays and Etta James, though no one was as important to Michael as James Brown. "I knew every step, every grunt, every spin and turn," he recalled. "He would give a performance that would exhaust you, just wear you out emotionally. His whole physical presence, the fire coming out of his pores, would be phenomenal. You'd feel every bead of sweat on his face, and you'd know what he was going through.…You couldn't teach a person what I've learned just standing and watching."

The most famous site on these tours was the Apollo in New York, where the Jackson 5 won an Amateur Night show in 1967. Joe had invested everything he had in his sons' success, though of

RIDING HIGH
The Jackson 5 with Diana Ross in 1970. A year earlier, Motown moved the family to L.A., set them up at the homes of Ross and label head Berry Gordy, and began grooming them for stardom.

course any real recognition or profit would be his success as well. While on the circuit, Joe had come to know Gladys Knight, who was enjoying a string of small successes with Motown, America's pre-eminent black pop label. With the encouragement of both Knight and Motown R&B star Bobby Taylor, Joe took his sons to Detroit to audition for the label. In 1969, Motown moved the Jackson family to Los Angeles, set them up at the homes of Diana Ross and the label's owner, Berry Gordy, and began grooming them. Michael remembered Gordy telling them, "I'm gonna make you the biggest thing in the world.... Your first record will be a Number One, your second record will be a Number One, and so will your third record. Three Number One records in a row."

IN 1959, GORDY FOUNDED TAMLA RECORDS – WHICH soon became known as Motown – in Detroit. By the time he signed the Jackson 5, Motown had long enjoyed its status as the most important black-owned-and-operated record label in America, spawning the successes of Smokey Robinson and the Miracles, the Temptations, Mary Wells, the Four Tops, and Diana Ross and the Supremes, among others. In contrast to Stax and Atlantic, Motown's soul wasn't especially bluesy or gritty, nor was it a music that spoke explicitly to social matters or to the black struggle in the U.S. By its nature the label exemplified black achievement, but its music was calibrated for assimilation by the pop mainstream – which of course meant a white audience as much as a black one (the label's early records bore the legend "The Sound of Young America"). At the time, rock music was increasingly becoming a medium for album-length works. By contrast, Motown maintained its identity as a factory that manufactured hit singles, despite groundbreaking albums by Stevie Wonder and Marvin Gaye. Gordy was looking for a singles-oriented group that would not only deliver hits for young people, but would also give them somebody to seize as their own, to identify with and to adore. The Jackson 5, Gordy said, would exemplify "bubblegum soul."

TIME OUT
Michael outside the family's Encino, California, home, circa 1973

The Jackson 5's first three singles – "I Want You Back," "ABC" and "The Love You Save" – became Number One hits as Gordy had promised, and so did a fourth, "I'll Be There." The group was established as the breakout sensation of 1970. Fred Rice, who would create Jackson 5 merchandise for Motown, said, "I call 'em the black Beatles.... It's unbelievable." And he was right. The Jackson 5 defined the transition from 1960s soul to 1970s pop as much as Sly and the Family Stone did, and at a time when many Americans were uneasy about minority aspirations to power, the Jackson 5 conveyed an agreeable ideal of black pride, one that reflected kinship and aspiration rather than opposition. They represented a realization that the civil rights movement made possible, and that couldn't have happened even five or six years earlier. Moreover, the Jackson 5 earned critical respectability. Reviewing "I Want You Back" in ROLLING STONE, Jon Landau wrote, "The arrangement, energy and simple spacing of the rhythm all contribute to the record's spellbinding impact." And though they functioned as a group, there was no question who the

MOTOWN SUPERSTARS
Jackson in the studio with Stevie Wonder during the recording of "You Haven't Done Nothin'" in 1974. The Jacksons sang backup on the track.

Jackson 5's true star was, and who they depended on. Michael's voice also worked beyond conventional notions of male-soul vocals – even worked beyond gender. Cultural critic and musician Jason King, in an outstanding essay, recently wrote, "It is not an exaggeration to say that he was the most advanced popular singer of his age in the history of recorded music. His untrained tenor was uncanny. By all rights, he shouldn't have had as much vocal authority as he did at such a young age."

For at least the first few years, Michael and his brothers seemed omnipresent and enjoyed universal praise. But soon they experienced some hard limitations. The music they were making wasn't really of invention – they didn't write or produce it – and after Michael was relegated to recording throwback fare like "Rockin' Robin," in 1972, he worried that the Jackson 5 would become an "oldies act" before he left adolescence. The Jackson 5 began pushing to produce themselves and to create their own sound. Stevie Wonder and Marvin Gaye had demonstrated an ability to grow and change – and sell records – when given creative leeway, and with 1974's "Dancing Machine," the Jacksons proved they could thrive when they seized a funk groove. Motown, however, wouldn't consider it. "They not only refused to grant our requests," Michael said in *Moonwalk*, "they told us it was taboo to even mention that we wanted to do our own music." Michael understood what this meant: Not only would Motown not let the Jackson 5 grow, they also wouldn't let *him* grow. Michael bided his time, studying the producers he and his brothers worked with. "I was like a hawk preying in the night," he said. "I'd watch everything. They didn't get away with nothing without me seeing. I really wanted to get into it."

In 1975, Joe Jackson negotiated a new deal for his sons – this time with Epic Records, for a 500 percent royalty-rate increase. The contract also stipulated solo albums from the Jacksons (though the arrangement did not include Jermaine, who married Gordy's daughter Hazel and stayed with Motown, creating a rift with the family that lasted for several years). Motown tried to block the deal, and in the end stopped the brothers from using the Jackson 5 name; the group would now be known as the Jacksons. Epic initially placed them with Philadelphia producers Kenny Gamble and Leon Huff, but it wouldn't be until 1978's *Destiny* that the Jacksons finally seized control over their own music and recast their sound – sexy and smooth in the dance-floor hits "Blame It on the Boogie" and the momentous "Shake Your Body (Down to the Ground)," and reflecting a new depth and emotional complexity in songs like "Push Me Away" and "Bless His Soul."

Destiny, though, was merely a prelude: By the time the album was finished, Michael was ready to make crucial changes that would establish his ascendancy as a solo artist. He fired his father as his manager and in effect found himself a new father, producer Quincy Jones, whom Michael connected with while filming *The Wiz* (a reworking of *The Wizard of Oz*). Jones was a respected jazz musician, bandleader, composer and arranger who had worked with Clifford Brown, Frank Sinatra, Lesley Gore, Count Basie, Aretha Franklin and Paul Simon, and he had written the film scores for *The Pawnbroker, In Cold Blood*

and *In the Heat of the Night.* Jackson liked the arranger's ear for mixing complex hard beats with soft overlayers. "It was the first time that I fully wrote and produced my songs," Jackson said later, "and I was looking for somebody who would give me that freedom, plus somebody who's unlimited musically." Specifically, Jackson said his solo album had to sound different than the Jacksons; he wanted a cleaner and funkier sound. The pairing proved as fortuitous as any collaboration in history. Jones brought an ethereal buoyancy to Jackson's soft erotic fever on songs like "Rock With You" and "Don't Stop 'Til You Get Enough," and in a stunning moment like "She's Out of My Life," Jones had the good sense to let nothing obscure the magnificent heartbreak in the singer's voice. The resulting album, *Off the Wall* – which established Jackson as a mature artistic force in his own right – has the most unified feel of any of his works. It was also a massive hit, selling more than 5 million copies in the U.S. alone by 1985.

Michael Jackson had in effect become one of the biggest black artists America had ever produced, and he expected *Off the Wall* to win top honors during the 1980 Grammy Awards ceremony. Instead, it received only one honor, for Best Male R&B Vocal. The Doobie Brothers' "What a Fool Believes" won for Record of the Year, and Billy Joel's *52nd Street* won Album of the Year. Jackson was stunned and bitter. "My family thought I was going crazy because I was weeping so much about it," he recalled. "I felt ignored and it hurt. I said to myself, 'Wait until next time' – they won't be able to ignore the next album....That experience lit a fire in my soul."

Jackson told Jones – and apparently others as well – that his next album wouldn't simply be bigger than *Off the Wall*, it would be the biggest album ever. When *Thriller* was released in November 1982, it didn't seem to have any overarching theme or even a cohesive style. Instead, it sounded like an assembly of singles – like a greatest-hits album, before the fact. But it became evident fast that this was exactly what Jackson intended *Thriller* to be: a brilliant collection of songs intended as hits, each one designed with mass crossover audiences in mind. Jackson put out "Billie Jean" for the dance crowd, "Beat It" for the white rockers, and then followed each crossover with crafty videos designed to enhance both his allure and his inaccessibility. Yet after hearing these songs find their natural life on radio, it was obvious that they were something more than exceptional highlights. They were a well-conceived body of passion, rhythm and structure that defined the sensibility – if not the inner life – of the artist behind them. These were instantly compelling songs about emotional and sexual claustrophobia, about hard-earned adulthood and about a newfound brand of resolution that worked as an arbiter between the artist's fears and the inescapable fact of his fame. "Wanna Be Startin' Somethin'" had the sense of a vitalizing nightmare in its best lines ("You're stuck in the middle/And the pain is thunder....Still they hate you, you're a vegetable....They eat off you, you're a vegetable"). "Billie Jean," in the meantime, exposed the ways in which the interaction between the artist's fame and the outside world might invoke soul-killing dishonor ("People always told me, be careful of what you do....'Cause the lie becomes the truth," Jackson sings, possibly

FLYING SOLO
Jackson in Jamaica in 1975, the year he released his
fourth solo album, "Forever, Michael." It was his last
Motown LP – the brothers left for Epic shortly after.

thinking of a paternity charge from a while back). And "Beat It" was pure anger – a rousing depiction of violence as a male stance, as a social inheritance that might be overcome. In sum, *Thriller*'s parts added up to the most improbable kind of art – a work of personal revelation that was also a mass-market masterpiece. It's an achievement that will likely never be topped.

Except, in a sense, Jackson did top it, and he did it within months after *Thriller*'s release. It came during a May 16th, 1983, TV special celebrating Motown's 25th anniversary. Jackson had just performed a medley of greatest hits with his brothers. It was exciting stuff, but for Michael it wasn't enough. As his brothers said their goodbyes and left the stage, Michael remained. He seemed shy for a moment, trying to find words to say. "Yeah," he almost whispered, "those were good old days.... I like those songs a lot. But especially—" and then he placed the microphone into the stand with a commanding look and said, "I like the new songs." He swooped down, picked up a fedora, put it on his head with confidence and vaulted into "Billie Jean." This was one of Michael Jackson's first public acts as a star outside and beyond the Jacksons, and it was startlingly clear that he was not only one of the most thrilling live performers in pop music, but that

he was perhaps more capable of inspiring an audience's imagination than any single pop artist since Elvis Presley. There are times when you know you are hearing or seeing something extraordinary, something that captures the hopes and dreams popular music might aspire to, and that might unite and inflame a new audience. That time came that night, on TV screens across the nation – the sight of a young man staking out his territory, and just starting to lay claim to his rightful pop legend. "Almost 50 million people saw that show," Jackson wrote in *Moonwalk*. "After that, many things changed."

He was right. That was the last truly blessed moment in Michael Jackson's life. After that, everything became argument and recrimination. And in time, decay.

BEFORE GOING INTO THAT AREA – WHERE THE story breaks in two – it's probably worth asking, What kind of person was Michael Jackson at that time? What were his hopes and his problems? What did he want his music to say or accomplish? How did he relate to the audience who loved him, and how did he relate to himself? Up to this point, these questions haven't really figured; Michael Jackson was an immensely talented young man – he seemed shy but ambitious, and he certainly seemed enigmatic. Nobody knew much about his beliefs or his sex life; he rarely gave interviews, but he also didn't land himself in scandals. He did, however, describe himself as a lonely person – particularly around the time he made *Off the Wall*. Former *Los Angeles Times* music critic Robert Hilburn recently wrote of meeting Jackson in 1981, when the singer was 23, that Jackson struck him as "one of the most fragile and lonely people I've ever met…almost abandoned. When I asked why he didn't live on his own like his brothers, instead remaining at his parents' house, he said, 'Oh, no, I think I'd die on my own. I'd be so lonely. Even at home, I'm lonely. I sit in my room and sometimes cry. It is so hard to make friends, and there are some things you can't talk to your parents or family about. I sometimes walk around the neighborhood at night, just hoping to find someone to talk to. But I just end up coming home.'"

Jackson's social uneasiness was probably formed by the wounds in his history; the children were insulated from others their age, and Jackson's status as a lifelong star may have left him feeling not just cut off from most people, but also alien from them – as if his experience or his vocation made him extraordinary. "I hate to admit it," he once said, "but I feel strange around everyday people." Not exactly an unusual sentiment for some cloistered celebrities, especially former child stars. At the same time, it's a statement full of signals: Jackson didn't enjoy the sort of company that might guide him in positive ways. He probably never did, throughout his life. Maybe the most troubling passage in *Moonwalk* is when he talks about children in the entertainment world who eventually fell prey to drugs: "I can understand…considering the enormous stresses put upon them at a young age. It's a difficult life."

In any event, Michael Jackson seemed clearly reputable – eminent though not heroic, not yet messianic, and certainly not contemptible. *Thriller* placed seven singles in *Billboard*'s Top 10 and also became the biggest-selling album in history (presently around 50 million copies or more), and at the 1984 Grammy Awards, Jackson finally claimed his due, capturing eight awards, including Album of the Year and Record of the Year. Then, months later, it was announced that Michael would be setting out on a nationwide tour with the Jacksons. He hadn't wanted to undertake the venture but felt obliged ("Those were slim shoulders on which to place such burdens," he wrote of his lifelong family pressures). Clearly, his talents and aspirations went beyond the limitations that his family act imposed on him. By all rights, he should have been taking the stage alone at that point in his career.

Jackson's aversion to the *Victory* tour was apparent when he sat looking miserable at press conferences or when he had to denounce statements by his father that he interpreted as casting aspersions on the Jacksons' management team of Ron Weisner and Freddy DeMann. "There was a time," Joe said, "when I felt I needed white help in dealing with the corporate power structure at CBS.…And I thought [Weisner-DeMann] would be able to help." Michael fired back furiously in a written comment to

Billboard: "To hear him talk like that turns my stomach. I don't know where he gets that from. I happen to be colorblind. I don't hire color; I hire competence.…I am president of my organization, and I have the final word on every decision. Racism is not my motto." It was the end of any lingering business relationship between Michael and his father.

It was during this period that a backlash first set in against Jackson, though from the press more than from the public. Actually, it began before the tour, as it became apparent that *Thriller* was headed for unprecedented sales at a blinding rate. The mid-1980s was a time when many in the music press had misgivings about mass popularity – especially if it seemed to represent a homogenized or acquiescent culture. Michael Jackson, after all, wasn't an artist with a message of sociopolitical revolution, nor did his lyrics reflect literary aspirations. To some then – and to some now – he represented little more than an ambition for personal fame. He wasn't, it seemed, an artist who would accomplish for his audience what Elvis Presley and the Beatles accomplished for theirs: the sort of event or disruption that changed both youth culture and the world. In my mind, Michael Jackson, Presley and the Beatles all shared one virtue: They bound together millions of otherwise dissimilar people in not just a quirk of shared taste, but also a forceful, heartfelt consensus that spoke to common dreams and values.

But there was a trickier concern at play. The racial dimensions of Jackson's image proved complex beyond any easy answers at

SOLITARY MAN
"I sit in my room and sometimes cry," Jackson said in 1981. "I sometimes walk around the neighborhood at night, just hoping to find someone to talk to."

that time, or even since. Some of that was attributable to charges that Jackson seemed willing to trade his former black constituency for an overwhelmingly white audience – otherwise how could he have achieved such staggering sales figures in the U.S.? But what probably inspired these race-related arguments most – the terrain where they all seemed to play out – was the topography of Jackson's face. With the exception of later accusations about his sexual behavior, nothing inspired more argument or ridicule about Michael Jackson than that face.

In his childhood, Jackson had a sweet, dark-skinned countenance; many early Jackson 5 fans regarded him as the cutest of the brothers. J. Randy Taraborrelli, author of *Michael Jackson: The Magic and the Madness*, has written, "[Michael] believed his skin…'messed up my whole personality.' He no longer looked at people as he talked to them. His playful personality changed and he became quieter and more serious. He thought he was ugly – his skin was too dark, he decided, and his nose too wide. It was no help that his insensitive father and brothers called him 'Big Nose.'" Also, as Jackson became an adolescent, he was horribly self-conscious about acne. Hilburn recalled going through a stack of photos with Jackson one night and coming across a picture of him as a teenager: "'Ohh, that's horrible,' [Jackson] said, recoiling from the picture."

The face Jackson displayed on the cover of *Thriller* had changed; the skin tone seemed lighter and his nose thinner and

straighter. In *Moonwalk*, Jackson claimed that much of the apparent renovation was due to a change in his diet; he admitted to altering his nose and his chin, but he denied he'd done anything to his skin. Still, the changes didn't end there. Over the years, Jackson's skin grew lighter and lighter, his nose tapered more and more, and his cheekbones seemed to gain prominence. To some, this all became fair game for derision; to others, it seemed a grotesque mutilation – not just because it might have been an act of conceit, aimed to keep his face forever childlike, but more troublingly because some believed Jackson wanted to transform himself into a white person. Or an androgyne – somebody with both male and female traits. The film *Three Kings* has a famous scene where an Iraqi interrogator asks a captured American soldier, "What is the problem with Michael Jackson? Your country make him chop up his face. . . . Michael Jackson is pop king of sick fucking country." The soldier replies, "It's bullshit – he did it to himself," and the Iraqi smacks him on the head with a clipboard. "It is so obvious. A black man make the skin white and the hair straight, and you know why? . . . Your sick fucking country make the black man hate hisself."

IN 1985, JAMES BALDWIN WROTE IN AN ESSAY FOR *Playboy*, "The Michael Jackson cacophony is fascinating in that it is not about Jackson at all. I hope he has the good sense to know it and the good fortune to snatch his life out of the jaws of a carnivorous success. He will not swiftly be forgiven for having turned so many tables, for he damn sure grabbed the brass ring, and the man who broke the bank at Monte Carlo has nothing on Michael. All that noise is about America, as the dishonest custodian of black life and wealth; and blacks, especially males, in America, and the burning, buried American guilt; and sex and sexual roles and sexual panic; money, success and despair. . . . "

Baldwin's paragraph was sympathetic and unflinching, but it was also prescient. Michael Jackson certainly wanted to seize the ring twice: He wanted his next album to be bigger than *Thriller*, which was of course too much to ask. An associate of his told me in 1988, "Michael still wants the world to acknowledge him." Maybe just as important, Jackson was also seeking vindication. He felt misjudged and maligned by much of the criticism heaped on him after the 1984 *Victory* tour. He had long been taught, by both his father and Motown, that the press was a vindictive force when it came to entertainers, that it reveled in the rhythm of building a celebrity's image, only to turn around and undermine that same person. In his case, Jackson wasn't half-wrong. Some of the scrutiny he received about his "freakishness" – his devotion to his animals as if they were his friends, his ongoing facial reconstruction, scornful charges that he slept in a hyperbaric oxygen chamber to maintain his youthfulness – was judgmental, even moralistic. Worse, too much of it came from reporters and gossip columnists, even political commentators, who displayed little if any real appreciation for Jackson's music and little respect for the sheer genius of his work.

At that time, Jackson's art was still his best way of making a case for himself. In 1987, he released *Bad*, his much-anticipated successor to *Thriller*. If not as eventful and ingenious as *Off the Wall* and *Thriller*, *Bad* was as good as any album he ever made. It was taut and funky, it had snap and fever, it radiated rage and self-pity but also yearning for grace and transcendence – particularly in "Man in the Mirror," a song about accepting social and political responsibility, and about the artist negotiating his way back into the world. *Bad* sold millions and launched five Number One singles, three more than *Thriller*, but because it couldn't match the accomplishments of *Thriller*, it was viewed as a flop.

Jackson then staged his first solo tour later that year. On several nights, I saw him turn in inspiring performances that also served as timely reminders of a sometimes overlooked truth about him: Namely, that whatever his eccentricities, Michael Jackson acquired his fame primarily because of his remarkably intuitive talents as a singer and dancer – talents that were genuine and matchless and not the constructions of mere ambition or hype. Though he had the lithe frame of Fred Astaire, the mad inventiveness of Gene Kelly, the sexy agony of Jackie Wilson, the rhythmic mastery of James Brown – or of Sammy Davis Jr., for that matter – nobody else moved like Michael Jackson. Certainly nobody else broke open their moment in one daring physical display like Jackson. He didn't invent the moonwalk – that famous and impossible backward gliding movement from his *Motown 25* performance of "Billie Jean" – but it didn't matter. He had defined himself in that moment and dared anybody else to match it, and nobody ever did. During the *Bad*

VICTORY LAP
Jackson during the "Victory" tour, in 1984. He was at the height of his fame but still bound to his brothers.

tour, his moves were breathtaking, sometimes unexpected. In the opening parts of songs like "Bad" and "The Way You Make Me Feel," he seemed self-conscious and strained pulling off the songs' cartoonish notion of streetwise sexuality, and his overstated hip pops and crotch snatching came off as more forced than felt. And yet when the music revved up, all the artifice was instantly dispelled. Jackson became suddenly confident and pulled off startling, robotic hip-and-torso thrusts alongside slow-motion, sliding-mime moves that left the audience gasping. Watching those quirky moves, you realized that all that came from somewhere within. You realized Jackson's exceptional talent could not be completely separable from his eccentricity.

In 1988, he was again nominated for key Grammy Awards including Album of the Year, but he was up against hard competition. Artists like U2 and Prince had fashioned the most ambitious and visionary music of their careers – music that reflected the state of pop and the world in enlivening ways. More to the point, in 1988 there was suspicion among many observers that Jackson's season as pop's favorite son had passed. He would win no Grammys that year. In the ROLLING STONE Readers' poll, Jackson placed first in six of the readers' "worst of the year" categories (including "worst male singer"); in addition, The *Village Voice* Critics' Poll failed to mention Jackson's *Bad* in its selection of 1987's 40 best albums. This was a startling turnaround from four years before, when Jackson and his work topped the same polls in both publications.

THRILLER
*Jackson at an amusement park
in Cologne, Germany, in 1987*

Michael Jackson never really regained momentum or ambition after the negative reaction to *Bad*. He had finally left the family home in Encino and built his own fortress estate known as Neverland, about 100 miles north of L.A., with an amusement park and train rides redolent of Disneyland. It became a place where he brought the world to him, or at least that part of the world he seemed to care about, which mainly included children – the people, he said, he felt most at home with, since part of him wanted to experience and share the childhood he felt his father and entertainment career had deprived him of. But it was also Michael's appetite for the company of children that would create the most lamentable troubles in his life. In 1993, a story broke that Jackson was accused of molesting a 13-year-old boy with whom he had kept frequent company. It was a serious accusation, and it forced Jackson to issue a public denial in video form. Given what many had long regarded as Jackson's oddness and his indeterminate sexuality – he had dated Tatum O'Neal and Brooke Shields, but it was unclear if he ever had romances with them – and given his fondness for the company of children, the charges seemed all too credible to many observers. The story played big not just in tabloid newspapers but in some mainstream media as well. No criminal charges were filed, and no other credible witnesses came forward, but in 1994 Jackson settled the matter out of court (reportedly for something in the vicinity of $20 million), which struck many as a tacit admission to the allegations. Jackson, though, categorically denied the claim. He later told British journalist Martin Bashir that he simply wanted to get the issue behind him.

The episode did enormous damage to Jackson's image, and perhaps to his psychology, as well. It was during that time that, according to some, he developed a dependency on medications that stayed with him through the rest of his life. (Jackson's need for drugs may also have stemmed from pains attributable to various surgeries.) That same year, he unexpectedly married Lisa Marie Presley, the daughter of rock & roll's most eminent pioneer, Elvis Presley. Some saw it as an effort to both rehabilitate and bolster his image by asserting a heterosexual authenticity, and by linking his name to even greater fame. The marriage lasted 20 months. Presley has never spoken negatively of Jackson, only affectionately, saying in the days after her ex-husband's death that she left him only because she felt she couldn't save him from himself. Jackson married again in 1996, this time to a nurse from his dermatologist's office, Debbie Rowe. The couple had two children, son Prince Michael Jackson and daughter Paris Michael Katherine Jackson. Apparently, the children were the true objective of the marriage for Jackson; the couple divorced in 1999, and Rowe gave up custody of the children. (Rowe has admitted in the past that Jackson wasn't the children's biological father, rather that they were conceived by artificial insemination.)

As a result of all this, what Michael Jackson became famous for changed, for the remainder of his life. He had already been seen, since the onset of his *Thriller*-born fame, as somebody who, in his own words, was "so weird and bizarre." This isn't to say Jackson's still-massive audience viewed him in those terms;

it's clear from the impassioned responses to his 1992-93 *Dangerous* tour – covering Europe, Latin America, the Middle East and Asia – that Jackson still stood as a potent and vastly loved symbol of artistic and racial transcendence for his audience. But in the eyes of much American media, Jackson was regarded after the 1993 scandal as something worse than an oddity: a possible child abuser. The quality of his music, some thought, no longer mattered in comparison with what he had been accused of. It certainly didn't help matters that Jackson's public way of reacting to his newly maligned image was the same way he always promoted his persona: in grandiose terms. The cover art to his 1995 album, *HIStory: Past, Present and Future*, portrayed him as a towering statue, an icon beyond tarnish. With songs like "Black or White" and "Heal the World," from his 1991 album *Dangerous*, he had already been promoting himself as a force that wanted to save the world, not corrupt any part of it. For better or worse, the key emblem that confirmed his worthy intentions – at least in the videos for these songs and others – was the faces, the innocence, of children. Clearly, Jackson was either scorning those who had smeared him, by attempting to best their righteousness, or he was plain arrogant and reckless. Asserting himself as a demigod in the early 1990s seemed a disproportionate and out-of-touch reaction to the damaging reality he was now forced to live with.

But what is interesting is that this was also the time in which Jackson made some of his most interesting art: some of his wit-

MICHAEL ON TOP
Jackson in 1991, the year he released "Dangerous," which debuted at Number One on the "Billboard" album chart.

tiest, his most pain-filled, his angriest and by far his most politically explicit or troubling. Since Jackson's rise to phenomenal fame in the 1980s, a number of critics had taken the singer to task for failing to address more directly the social realities of the times, for reveling in his own gigantism rather than voicing the apprehensions in the world around him. He had addressed those recriminations somewhat with the anti-racism of "Black or White" ("Causing grief in/Human relations/It's a turf war/On a global scale") and in the generic altruism of "Heal the World." *HIStory*'s "They Don't Care About Us" was more forceful: "Am I invisible because you ignore me?/Your proclamation promised me free liberty, now/I'm tired of bein' the victim of shame/They're throwing me in a class with a bad name/I can't believe this is the land from which I came/You know I really do hate to say it/The government don't wanna see." The initial release of the song – with such lyrics as "Jew me, sue me/Everybody do me/Kick me, kike me" – was also problematic, and caused more unwanted trouble for Jackson. In June 1995, he told *The New York Times*, "The idea that these lyrics could be deemed objectionable is extremely hurtful to me, and misleading. The song in fact is about the pain of prejudice and hate and is a way to draw attention to social and political problems. I am the voice of the accused and the attacked. I am the voice of everyone. I am the skinhead, I am the Jew, I am the black man, I am the white man. I am not the one who was attacking. It is about the injustices to young people and how the system can wrongfully accuse them.

TRAGIC KINGDOM
*Jackson in 1993 at his
Neverland Ranch in Los
Olivos, California, which
included an amusement
park and zoo. "I'm just
putting behind the gates
everything I never got
to do as a kid," he said.*

I am angry and outraged that I could be so misinterpreted." He also told ABC News interviewer Diane Sawyer, "It's not anti-Semitic because I'm not a racist person."

HIStory's best new material represented Jackson as a changed man and artist: somebody both mature but defensive; somebody loving (his video moments with Lisa Marie Presley seem surprisingly tender, sincere and sexy), but also bitterly wounded and spiteful. Songs like "D.S." (a thinly veiled screed against prosecutor Tom Sneddon) and "Tabloid Junkie" equated Jackson's accusers with social wrongdoers and despite the fallacy, proved even more convincing as angry rock & roll. In the far more treacly "Childhood," he put forth his case for his otherness: "No one understands me/They view it as such strange eccentricities. . . . It's been my fate to compensate/For the childhood I've never known. . . . Before you judge me, try hard to love me/Look within your heart, then ask/Have you seen my childhood?" Two years later, though, still dismayed at how the media continued to judge him, Jackson lashed out in "Is It Scary," a song from his 1997 remix album, *Blood on the Dance Floor*: "Am I the beast you visualized/And if you wanna see/Eccentric oddities/I'll be grotesque before your eyes. . . . So tell me . . . am I scary for you?"

MICHAEL JACKSON'S HURT AND ANGER continued to come out in his body more over the years. Sometimes the expression we saw from him in public looked terrified, his eyes peering over surgical masks or from behind the cover of a burqa. Other times, in both his videos and stage performances, he moved with an explosive fury. There are no doubt many reasons Michael Jackson transformed himself physically. His claims to a skin-lightening condition, according to his dermatologist, were in fact true and drove much of his transformation, though his increasing obsession with unending physical renovation drove it just as much. No matter what many of us thought of the psychology that produced all this, and the damage that resulted, it is also true that the person that Michael Jackson turned himself into wasn't simply pathetic or miscast: He was a work of physical self-creation unlike any we've ever seen. It's possible that he could not even have written the songs he did past the 1980s had he not remade himself. "Black or White" included the rap "Where your blood/Comes from/Is where your space is/I've seen the bright/Get duller/I'm not going to spend/My life being a color."

Despite all this, though, Michael Jackson's 1990s music had less presence in the ongoing current of popular culture. His final album, *Invincible*, from 2001, yielded more adventurous tracks – Jackson was finally accommodating the stylistic and cultural innovations made by hip-hop and other urban music forms – but overall it wasn't enough to live up to its title. This isn't to say that Michael Jackson was no longer a huge star, but rather that his legend had transmuted: He was now known for his excesses and bad choices. He lived in a castle; he contracted another baby, Prince Michael II (whose mother has never been identified); and he then recklessly dangled the baby over a balcony in Berlin. Sometimes you had to wonder whether Jackson had any real idea how his actions struck the world – which is perhaps OK, unless you expect the world to love you unconditionally.

JACKSON'S MOST EGREGIOUS LAPSE OF JUDGMENT became evident in a notorious 2003 interview with Martin Bashir, in which the singer professed that he still shared his bed at Neverland with children who were not his own. During one point in the broadcast, Jackson sat holding the hand of a 13-year-old boy, a cancer survivor, and explained what he saw as the innocent and loving nature of that behavior. The public response was swift and hypercritical; many thought that despite the accusations he had faced in 1993, Jackson could still act as he wanted with impunity. The reaction was so devastating to Jackson that, according to some rumors, later that year he attempted a morphine overdose; at the very least, some observers declared Jackson had committed career suicide. The controversy became as serious as possible when the boy in the video accused Jackson of fondling him. This time, the matter went to trial. The horrible drama that Jackson had landed in was in keeping with the dominant themes of his life and art: his obsessions with stardom, mystery, hubris, fear and despoiled childhood. If the charges were true, one had to wonder what Jackson truly saw when he looked at the childhoods of others. Was he capable of disrespecting their innocence, just as his own was once ruined? But if the charges weren't true, then one had to ask what measure of satisfaction could be won in his ruin?

The 2005 trial was the spectacle everybody expected it to be – a drama about justice and celebrity, sex and outrage, morality and race. Even though it dragged on, it was clear the prosecution didn't have a case so much as it had umbrage. The trial was a farce – it's dismaying the case ever made it to trial – and Jackson was acquitted on all charges. But the damage done seemed, in many ways, final. Jackson walked out of the courtroom that day a shaken, listless man. His finances were also coming undone; he had been spending ludicrous sums and he'd mismanaged his money – which took some doing, since he had made such a vast fortune. The biggest star in the world had fallen from the tallest height. He left the country and moved to Bahrain; he was only occasionally seen or heard from. Nobody knew whether he could recover his name, or even preserve his considerable music legacy, until early 2009, when he announced an incredibly ambitious series of 50 concerts – which he described as the "final curtain call" – to take place at London's O$_2$ arena, beginning July 13th.

It's hard to believe that Jackson, who was so proud of his public performances and so peerless at delivering them, would have committed himself to a project in which he might fail so tremendously. At the same time, it is not inconceivable that Michael Jackson could have been a man half-hungry and broken in his last few years. All that is certain is that on June 25th, 2009, in Los Angeles, Michael Jackson met the only sure redemption he might know, in the most famous unexpected death in current history. That redemption didn't come because he died, but because his death forced us to reconsider what his life added up to.

COURT JESTER
*Jackson outside a Santa Maria, California,
courthouse in January 2004, after his arraignment
on child-molestation charges.*

What killed Michael Jackson? His lifelong pursuit of fame and vindication? No doubt, in part. He pushed too hard, wanted too much; he didn't recognize limitations. The pain of achieving so much yet being derided and dismissed time and again had to be considerable. It's also clear that all the hatred and judgment directed his way for his peculiarities and for his rumored sexual behavior had to debilitate his spirit, if not his body. That subject of child molestation will always, of course, be a crux concern about his life, one that, for many people, clearly – and understandably – trumps his art. We will likely never know what the truth was, which is one more awful aspect of the whole nightmare. The accusation will always stay attached to his name.

What, then, saved Michael Jackson – that is, after his death? At the least, his art and his accomplishments. When somebody makes as much great music as Jackson did, our collective pleasures are enriched and our history is made more intense and complex. In his ambitions, in his setbacks and most important, in his sounds, he embodied black music history in America. But he did more: The barriers he broke helped make the modern pop world a more inclusive scene than it once was before. That is, he staked out new territory. It is always a good thing to see some-body transforming the world of known possibilities. I remember, as a kid, watching Elvis Presley do it on the Dorsey brothers' *Stage Show* and *The Ed Sullivan Show*. I remember, as an adolescent, watching the Beatles open up whole new artistic and historic possibilities in their first U.S. appearances, live on *Ed Sullivan*. I remember, in my first year as a writer for ROLLING STONE, watching the Sex Pistols crack old surfaces and yield a new future – even as they sang of "no future" onstage at San Francisco's Winterland, during their last 1970s performance.

Still, I'll never forget that night back in early 1983, when on-stage in Pasadena, California, at the Motown 25th-anniversary show, Michael Jackson gave his first public performance as a mature artist staking his own claim, vaulting into that astonishingly graceful, electrifying version of "Billie Jean." Dancing, spinning, sending out impassioned, fierce glares at the overcome audience, Jackson did a powerful job of animating and mythologizing his own blend of mystery and sexuality. I'd never seen anything quite like it before. Maybe I never will again. Michael Jackson didn't just grab the gold ring: He hooked it to a new bar and set it even higher, and nobody has yet snatched it with quite the same flair or results.

FINAL CURTAIN CALL
Jackson's last concert rehearsal at L.A.'s Staples Center on June 23rd, 2009, two days before he died. Jackson spent three months rehearsing for his 50-date stand at London's O₂ arena.

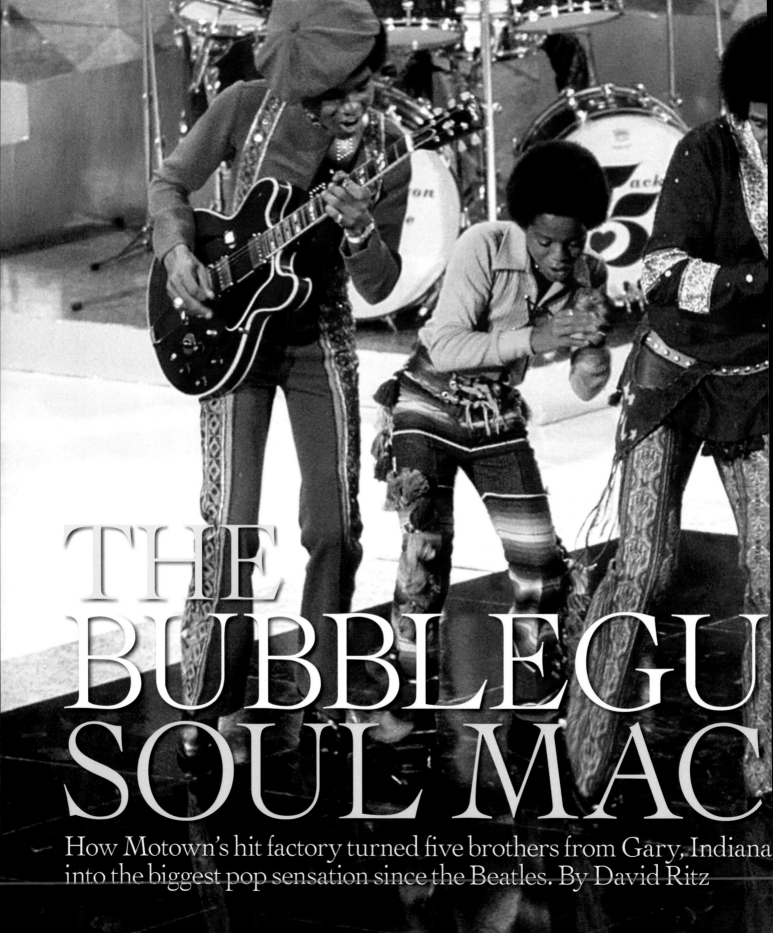

THE BUBBLEGU
SOUL MAC

How Motown's hit factory turned five brothers from Gary, Indiana
into the biggest pop sensation since the Beatles. By David Ritz

M
HINE

IN THE SUMMER OF 1968, A NINE-YEAR-OLD MICHAEL JACKSON, BACKED BY HIS OLDER brothers Jackie, Tito, Jermaine and Marlon, took the stage of the Regal Theater in Chicago. The Jackson 5 were opening for Motown R&B act Bobby Taylor and the Vancouvers (with Tommy Chong, later of Cheech and Chong, on guitar), who were riding high on their hit single "Does Your Mama Know About Me." Taylor was watching from the wings. "This squirt did James Brown better than JB himself," he recalls. "He broke out in 'Cold Sweat.' He sang 'I Got the Feelin' with feelings you can't fake. He tore up the stage like JB's long-lost love child – the spins, the mike action, the fall-on-your-knees-and-beg-for-it moves. His voice grabbed me by the throat and said, 'Take me to your heart. Take me to your leader.' So right after the show, I did just that. I jumped up and told his dad, 'Joe, we're off to Detroit.'"

Three years earlier, the Gary, Indiana, group had begun winning local talent contests with Motown covers like the Temptations' "My Girl." Joe turned the tiny family home at 2300 Jackson Street into a rehearsal hall. "The simple mathematics of our living situation," said mother Katherine, "11 human beings, a two-bedroom house, made us a curiosity in the neighborhood."

At the time of the Regal show, the Jackson 5 had cut a single on a local label, and Joe Jackson was planning to take his sons to New York. "But Bobby Taylor was one of those headstrong guys who wouldn't take no for an answer," Joe said. "He was cocky, but you had to respect him because he sang his ass off. He also said that he knew [Motown chief] Berry Gordy personally, and, if he had to, he'd tie him up in a chair and make him listen to us."

Taylor brought the group to stay with him in Detroit that night. Gordy was in L.A., where he was planning to move Motown. "We filmed Mike doing his James Brown thing and flew a copy to the coast," says Taylor. "Next day, Berry was on the line: 'Sign them. Sign them now!' Later, I started cutting tracks and teaching 'em songs."

With Taylor producing, the Jackson 5 began recording their debut album in Detroit that summer. At the time, the Motown machine was pumping out hits like bumpers at the Ford plant, with nonstop smashes from the Miracles, the Supremes, the Temptations, the Four Tops and Stevie Wonder. The year the brothers signed to Motown, the label had nine Number One hits – including Marvin Gaye's scorching "I Heard It Through the Grapevine," which became the biggest-selling single in Motown history up to that time.

"I was hanging around the studio in Detroit," Gaye remembered in a 1983 interview, "and heard this sound coming out of the rooms. Someone was singing 'Who's Lovin' You.' I looked inside and saw five kids harmonizing into one mike. The littlest was so short he was standing on a milk crate. He was the one singing lead. Couldn't believe it. Crazy Bobby Taylor was in there producing. 'Hey, Marvin,' said Bobby, who loved to aggravate me, 'meet Michael Jackson. He'll be topping you in about a week.'"

"I saw the J5 as a straight-up soul group," says Taylor. "That's what I knew and loved – and that's what they knew and loved.

Mike went to bed with James Brown and Jackie Wilson records under his pillow. The rest of the brothers idolized Smokey and Marvin. The Jackson brothers, like their old man, were products of the great tradition. It was in my blood – and theirs – to cherish that tradition while taking it to the next level. It was my job to feed Mike's soul."

Clarence Paul, the late Motown producer-composer who was Little Stevie Wonder's conductor and surrogate dad, remembered Michael taking an avid interest in Motown's recording process. "He watched us like a hawk, and it didn't take him more than a hot minute to understand how the studio worked," he said. "One day he showed up while I was putting together background parts with the Andantes. I loved laying on thick harmony. I'd go to the piano and pick out the notes for the girls. When Mike saw what I was doing, he started singing each distinct part before I even got to the piano. He heard the whole harmonic range in his head and began singing every one of those separate lines. Instead of me showing him, he started showing me."

The Temptations' David Ruffin, among the greatest soul singers of any era, remembered finding Michael sitting in the corner of a Detroit studio: "Someone said, 'That's the Jackson kid.' I asked him if he wanted to sing with me. He said, 'Sure, Mr. Ruffin.' Well, he got up there and shadowed every last lick of mine. It was uncanny. If I did a fancy vocal run, he'd come back with one even fancier. He was copping from me, but also adding licks I hadn't even thought of. Joking around, I said, 'We could go on the road like Sam and Dave.' He said, 'You have to ask my father.' I remember thinking that for a boy who wanted to learn to be the best, God had put him in the absolutely pitch-perfect place."

Gordy's label was responsible for dozens of soul's greatest records, and by the late 1960s Motown was even more aggressively pursuing the larger, richer white market, signing acts, like the J5, with broad pop appeal. The Motown slogan read "The Sound of Young America" – the word "black" went unmentioned. "When we promoted our acts in the Sixties," explained Michael Roshkind, a former high-ranking Motown exec, "we explicitly avoided the word 'soul.' We wanted pop. You'll notice how decades later when Michael hit his stride around the world, he didn't name himself King of Soul.

He crowned himself King of Pop. He got that pop fixation from Berry."

In late 1968, Gordy invited the Jackson 5 to play at his Boston Boulevard mansion in Detroit. "There were skeptics," Taylor remembers. "Cats were calling them the Jackson Jive. Well, by the time they finished their first song, those who came to scoff stayed to pray. Berry said, 'Bring the boys to Hollywood. Bring them now!'"

The West Coast move was monumental – for Motown and the Jackson 5. The group's debut album, begun in Detroit, underwent a transformation in L.A. – and the sound that sent Michael soaring would be sculpted in Hollywood, but not by Taylor. Legendary Motown producer Hal Davis had been hired to set up a small office at Sunset and Vine. In 1996, Davis described Taylor's demise: "One night Bobby had Michael in the studio singing Clyde McPhatter's 'Money Honey' when Berry walked in. Berry told Bobby he was making a mistake by restricting them to R&B. Berry wanted pop songs. In his spitfire manner, Bobby gave Berry the finger. Then Berry gave Bobby the boot."

With Taylor gone, Gordy assigned his ace lieutenant, Suzanne de Passe, to manage the boys, while appointing himself commander in chief of an operation whose single mission was to make the Jackson 5 superstars. "In the summer of 1969, Berry was staying in the Hollywood Hills," Davis remembered, "and Diana Ross was living down the street. Half the brothers stayed with Berry, and the others, including Michael, stayed with Diana."

In *To Be Loved*, Gordy's autobiography, he describes that summer: "In some ways, the three-ring circus that took over my home . . . reminded me of the old days at Hitsville. Music vibrating throughout the house, writing sessions on the floor of the living room, pep talks in the kitchen while eating, rehearsals through the midnight hours, impromptu baseball games at the nearby park, swimming, shooting pool, basketball. Camaraderie, creativity and, of course, competition."

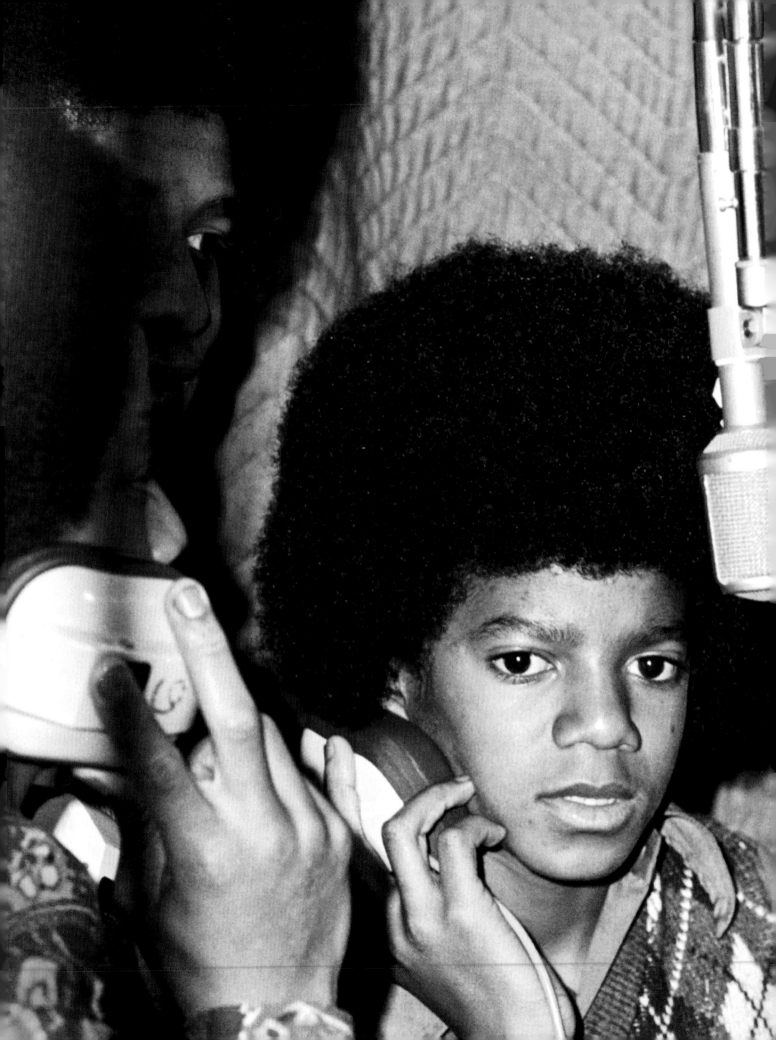

WONDER BOYS
Michael and his brothers in a Hollywood studio in 1974, the year "Dancing Machine" brought them back to the Top 10. The Jackson 5 played stints in Las Vegas and Senegal that year.

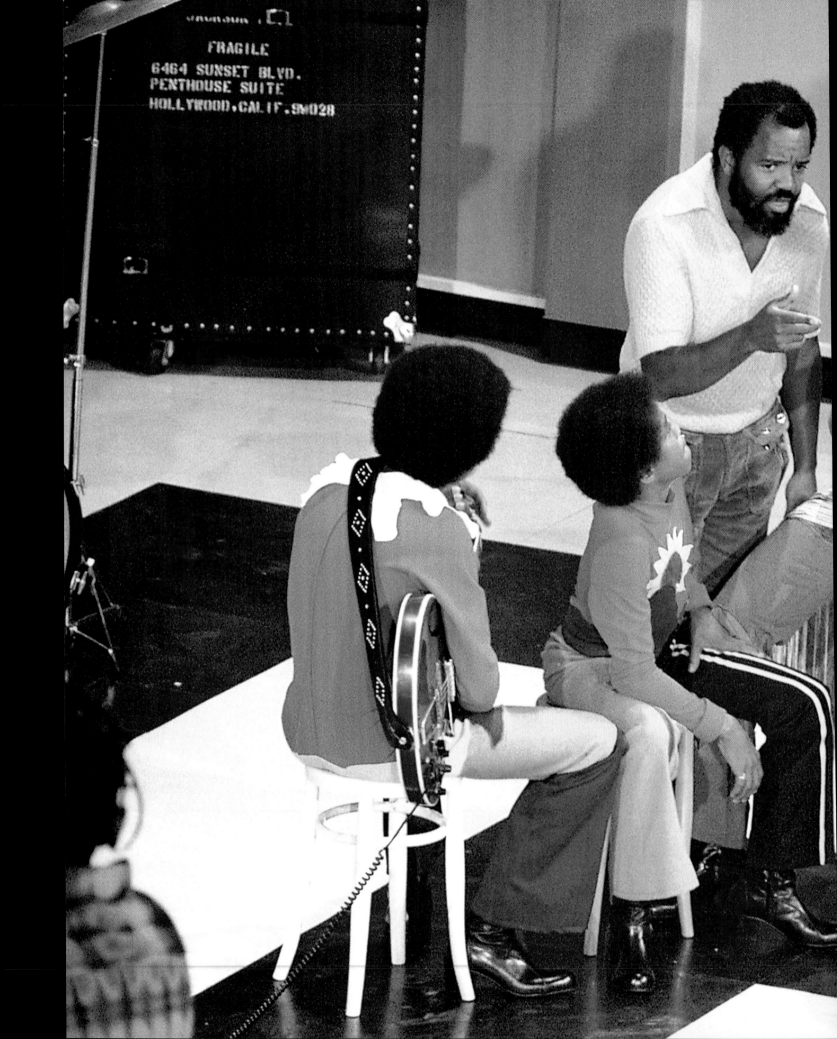

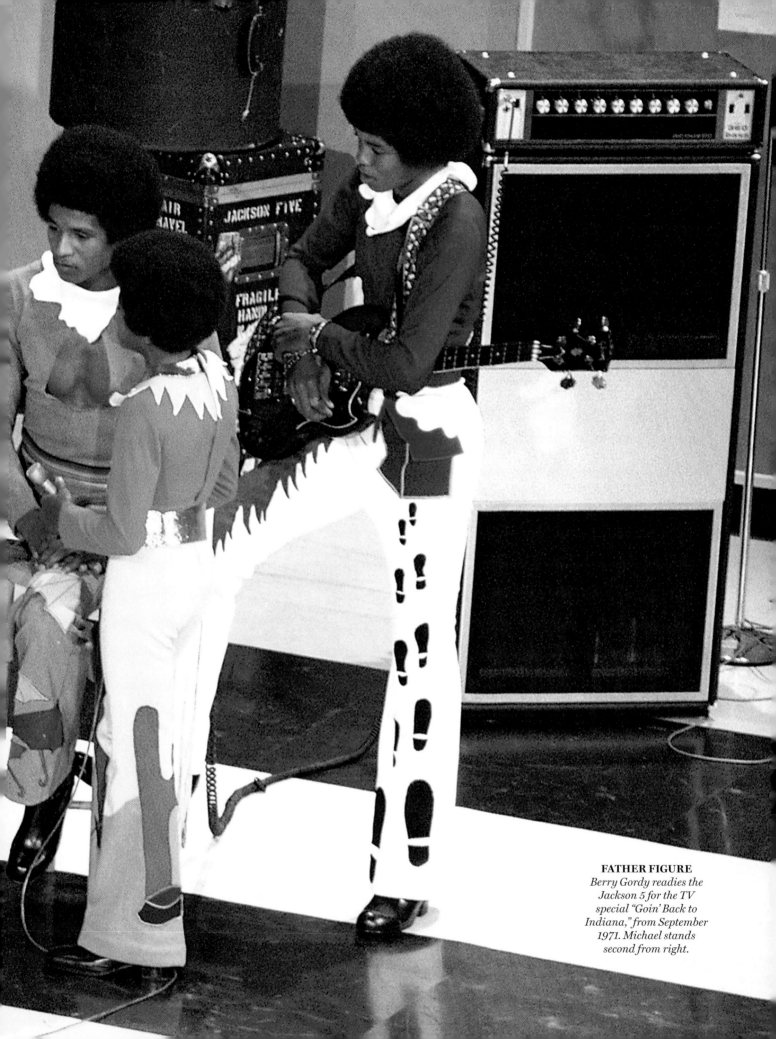

FATHER FIGURE
Berry Gordy readies the Jackson 5 for the TV special "Goin' Back to Indiana," from September 1971. Michael stands second from right.

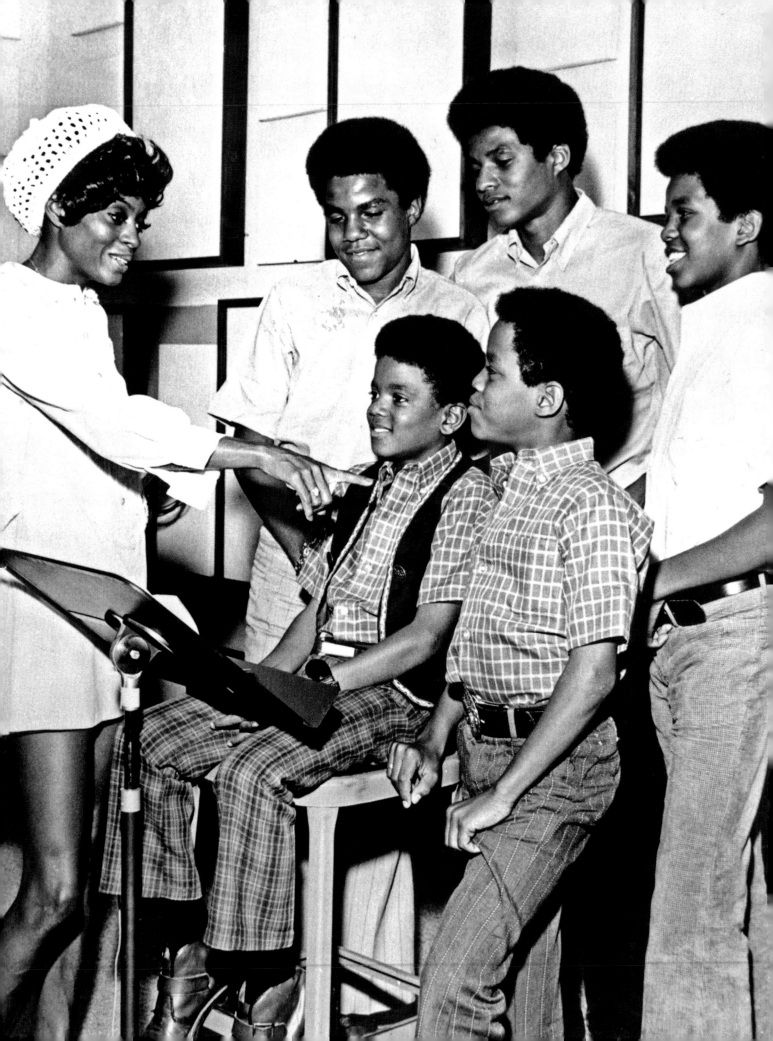

The brothers were given a tutor for their schoolwork named Rose Fine. They soon referred to her as their "Jewish mother." In his autobiography, *Moonwalk*, Michael wrote, "It was Rose who instilled in me a love of books and literature that sustains me today." He also underlined the public-relations training: "We had classes in manners and grammar. They gave us a list of questions, and they said they were the kinds of questions that we could expect people to ask us."

The grooming was intense, but not nearly as arduous as the recording sessions. The boys were shuffled in and out of studios seven days a week. In L.A., Gordy headed a "creative commando team" of songwriters and producers that he named the Corporation.

"Michael was interested in everything that had to do with singing and stage presentation," said Diana Ross. "He asked me how and why I chose songs. We talked about how songs tell stories, and how being a singer was like being an actor. I told him that if we were actors, Berry Gordy was our director and teacher. He was eager to be taught."

The Corporation – Berry, Deke Richards, Freddie Perren and Alphonso "Fonce" Mizell – understood that as the Sixties gave way to the Seventies, the towering figure in pop music was Sly Stone, and they wanted to capture the frenzied psychedelic funk of Sly's polypercussive playfulness. (Taylor knew this as well and, in fact, had recorded the Jackson 5 doing Sly's "Stand!") "The hip producers jumped on Sly's shit," said Etta James. "Those who didn't were left in the dust."

A LOVE SUPREME
Diana Ross was credited with "discovering" the J5 in 1969; Michael (seated) lived at her house in Hollywood that summer.

One of the first songs the Corporation crafted for the J5 was "I Wanna Be Free." According to Deke Richards, "We had Gladys Knight in mind, but Berry heard it for the J5." Gordy has a different memory. In 1994, he said, "I had this melody and little story going through my head for weeks. I kept singing, 'Oh, baby, give me one more chance.' The hook wouldn't leave me alone, and I always knew it was right for the boys. Deke, Freddie and Fonce added to it and worked it up into something much bigger."

The song became "I Want You Back." It hit the airwaves in the fall of 1969 and became the first of the Jackson 5's four straight Number One pop hits. During the previous months, the groundwork had been laid: Motown's PR machine spun a story that their most glamorous star, Diana Ross, had discovered the Jackson 5.

In August, they opened for the Supremes at the Forum; in October, they made their national TV debut on *The Hollywood Palace*, alongside Ross and Sammy Davis Jr. After the song's release, de Passe booked them on *Ed Sullivan*. By the summer of '70, America was awash in Jacksonmania.

"I Want You Back," followed by "ABC" and "The Love You Save," were the perfect vehicles for Michael's prepubescent charm. His piercing voice became an instrument of shocking clarity – proud, pleading, vulnerable. And the dance grooves were irresistible. The fourth in the Jackson 5's 11-month streak of Number One singles, "I'll Be There," produced by Hal Davis

and released in September 1970, raised the emotional stakes even higher. The boy was transformed into a man-child promising salvation and a lifetime of romantic devotion.

If the Supremes were girl-group chic, the Jackson 5 were boy-group cool, post-civil-rights-era well-mannered nice guys. Motown spun their wholesome image with just enough Hollywood flash – bell-bottoms as big as their Afros – to give them an edge. The brand extended to a Saturday-morning cartoon show, with the characters of Jackie, Jermaine, Tito, Marlon and Michael animated as fun-loving boys next door.

"To get those hits," said the late Hal Davis, "we probably had the boys record a hundred songs. Berry was unrelenting when it came to turning out product. His method was to breed fierce competition among the creative staff. That meant every songwriter and producer was working on J5 material. Everyone wanted a J5 cut. As a result, the boys never stopped running in and out of the studio. If you combine Berry's work ethic with Joe Jackson's, you understand Michael's workaholism."

Michael understood just how carefully the Motown machine was grooming him. In *Moonwalk*, he wrote about the press conferences following their first enormous wave of success: "Reporters would ask us all kinds of questions, and the Motown people would be standing by to help us out or monitor the questions. . . . Maybe they were worried after they gave us those Afros that they had created little Frankensteins. Once a reporter asked a Black Power question, and the Motown person told him we didn't think about that stuff because we were a 'commercial product.' It sounded weird, but we winked and gave the power salute when we left, which seemed to thrill the guy."

In 1971, barely 13, Michael Jackson recorded his first solo album, featuring three Top Five R&B hits: "Got to Be There," "Rockin' Robin" and "I Wanna Be Where You Are." His second, *Ben*, released just before his 14th birthday, was a huge hit. Michael sang the title song – about a boy who befriends a psychic rat – on the 1973 Academy Awards show. The single shot to Number One, proving Michael's remarkable ability to find poignancy in the macabre and ridiculousness in romance.

Bob Crewe, famous for his work with the Four Seasons, produced two Michael solo singles – "If n' I Was God" and the heartbreaking "To Make My Father Proud" – in 1973. "When I compare him to the other wonderful singers I've guided in the studio – Tina Turner, Patti Austin, Frankie Valli – I'd have to say that Michael was by far the easiest to direct," Crewe says. "Before I could offer any suggestions, he read my mind. He knew what I was thinking before I had the thought. He was miraculous."

"Is there a bad record Michael made for us?" Hal Davis asked himself. "In the years he was with Motown, I produced Michael more than anyone. But I'm telling you, there's nothing but sheer brilliance on those vocal tracks. He came singing like an angel – and left singing even better."

A case can be made for the superiority of Michael's Motown work to anything that follows. The argument rests on the almost frightening power of his pre-adolescent voice and the purity of his emotional output. Not yet a writer, he was an interpreter

who gave full heart to every musical story he sang. Later there would be subtext and nuance to his songwriting. But as he grew into a mature artist, he stood upon the sturdiest of foundations. Michael Jackson was first and foremost a Motown artist, an honor graduate of the most rigorous prep school pop music has ever known.

Decades later, Marvin Gaye reflected on the Michael saga: "Michael will never lose the quality that separates the merely sentimental from the truly heartfelt. It's rooted in the blues, and no matter what genre Michael is singing, that boy's got the blues."

"He's an ancient in modern times," Smokey Robinson observed. "I knew Jackie Wilson, I knew James Brown, I knew all the guys Michael loved. It took them years to develop their sound. Michael reminded me of Aretha. When Aretha was seven, she was playing full-chorded big-voiced gospel piano. That was a miracle. Michael was a miracle. In his heart, he carried other lifetimes. It was more than having soul; it was soul that went deep into the soil of a whole people's history."

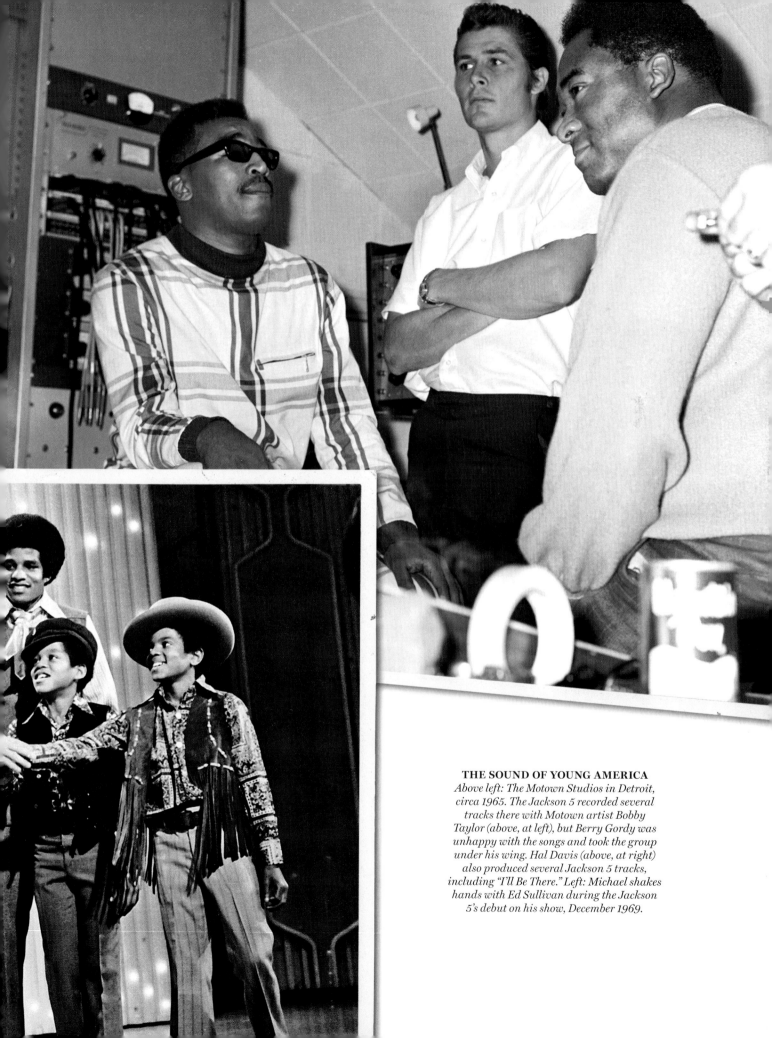

THE SOUND OF YOUNG AMERICA
Above left: The Motown Studios in Detroit, circa 1965. The Jackson 5 recorded several tracks there with Motown artist Bobby Taylor (above, at left), but Berry Gordy was unhappy with the songs and took the group under his wing. Hal Davis (above, at right) also produced several Jackson 5 tracks, including "I'll Be There." Left: Michael shakes hands with Ed Sullivan during the Jackson 5's debut on his show, December 1969.

JUMP FOR JOY
*Michael, Jermaine, Tito, Jackie
and Marlon Jackson (from left)
at their San Fernando Valley home
in 1971. The house had "only" six
bedrooms, so Michael had to share
with Marlon and Randy.*

LONDON TOWN
Michael leads his brothers at the Royal Variety Performance at London's Palladium, November 1st, 1972.

YOUNG GENIUS
*Michael, age 12,
in 1971*

THE PRINCE OF POP

Backstage jam sessions and hotel-room pillow
fights: On tour with Michael and the Jackson 5,
the hardest-working kids in show business
By Ben Fong-Torres

RS 81 · APRIL 29TH, 1971

When ROLLING STONE music editor Ben Fong-Torres hit the road
with the Jackson 5 for this 1971 cover story, it was an unusual as-
signment. "ROLLING STONE didn't do a whole lot of children's acts,"
Fong-Torres recalls. "But the music was just so extraordinary, and
it was popping all over the musical landscape – not just on Top 40
or soul radio but on FM rock stations." Fong-Torres spent four days
shadowing the group as it played shows in Columbus, Ohio, and its
hometown of Gary, Indiana. "They all talked about their ambitions,"
he says. "You'd think kids who had achieved what they achieved
would be glorying in it. Instead, they were all talking about going to
school to study business, music, acting or art." Looking back, Fong-
Torres has one major regret: On the cover – a striking image of
young Michael by ROLLING STONE photographer Henry Diltz – the
magazine posed the question WHY DOES THIS 11-YEAR-OLD STAY UP
PAST HIS BEDTIME? The problem? Michael was nearly 13 at the time
– Motown had shaved two years off his official age for PR reasons.

IN JANUARY 1971, THE JACKSON 5 ARE BACKSTAGE AT VETERANS MEMORIAL AUDIT-
orium in Columbus, Ohio, maybe 15 seconds before the call to go onstage. Michael Jackson is
making a request to Tito, who's diddling away on his electric guitar: "Play Brenda and the Tabula-
tions' song," he pleads. Tito, his serious face defiant beyond its 17 years, continues on the blues riff
he's found, way down at the bottom of the neck. Jermaine, on bass, is playing along, singing in his
new falsetto: "It's a sha-a-ame . . . the way you hurt me/Sha-a-ame . . . Ooh-ooh-ooh. . . . " Michael seems
restless, poking around the dull, well-lit dressing room in his stage outfit – an orange top with little green
turtles and a toga-style shoulder cape. After posing with his brothers for the local black paper – a dressing-
room ritual on this tour of the Midwest – he does his vocal exercises, hitting the high notes in little burps

while Jermaine is matching him on bass guitar. As 9:30 p.m. approaches, Michael asks Jack Nance, the road manager, for some food – especially a hot dog. Too late by a second; a man steps into the room and calls, "Let's go." Time to face 4,000 shrieks, and there is a remarkable lack of tension. Michael picks up a pair of sticks and begins drumming on a copy of ROLLING STONE with James Taylor on the cover until Marlon grabs the magazine.

"Let's go." By the time the Jacksons' band hits the "Stand" riff for the 12th time, the five brothers are up the ramp, past the columns of curtains and the first wave of screams, and lined up – tall Jackie in the center, Tito and Jermaine, behind their guitars, alongside, and Marlon and Michael on the wingtips. On a count, each puts one hand on his left hip, the other hand lightly cupping the right ear, and gets the right leg stomping, high-step style – all, of course, in unison, until Michael breaks away to take the mike and put his own voice above the screams.

THAT NIGHT, IN THEIR COLUMBUS HOTEL, the Jackson 5 are scattered among a couple of suites on the same floor (where, by the elevator, two security guards keep watch for persistent fans). A couple of them are playing cards with partially emptied glasses of milk and a bucket of the remains of fried chicken nearby. There is hard liquor, but it's being guzzled by the various promoters hanging around. Father Joe Jackson, watching the card game, remains quiet, except to help herd his sons over to talk.

Jackie, 19, talks about going to business school with an eye to "maybe take care of the financial part of the group someday." For now, "all I do is enjoy what I do onstage. It's something like a hobby." Tito, 17, is perhaps the most serious musician of the Jackson 5. He listens to Hendrix and B.B. King records. "Ever since I started playing guitar, about three years ago," he says. Tito shakes his head slowly, like an old bluesman reminiscing, when asked about the old days, seven years ago, when Michael first joined: "It was hard. Money was short. It was a drag." Jermaine, 16, laughs easily, with an open face and smile. After the initial introductions, he walks over, looks at my cassette recorder and asks, "Wanna talk right now?" He sits against the headboard of a bed; describes how he and his brothers go to a private school in Encino, California, five classrooms and 29 stu-

dents; how a tutor, assigned by the state board of education, follows them on their tours to keep them doing schoolwork.

Marlon, 13, is considered the quietest of the Jackson 5. At home, he shares a room with Michael and little Randy, and they play basketball and pool, and they swim. Marlon likes to watch cartoons Saturday mornings with Michael, and, like Michael, he's thinking of an acting career.

Michael Jackson is 11 years old, 75 pounds. And he's sung lead on almost all the Jackson 5's songs – six hit singles in 1970; three gold albums (plus a Christmas LP that is sure to play forever, like Bobby Helms' "Jingle Bell Rock"). And two hit singles so far this three-month-old year.

Michael sits on a couch in the hotel. He looks up, to indicate he's ready to be interviewed. He's done his two shows, and he's been relaxing – playing cards, doing card tricks and waiting for the inevitable pillow fight. So his brown eyes dart around now and then, watching for the first move.

He joined his brothers when he turned four; soon he perfected a James Brown imitation and made it his routine. "It was amazing," says Suzanne de Passe, who plans and coordinates the J5's stage show. "He had it down to a T" – every twist, turn, jerk and thrust. "And I had to work to get him away from a lot of it." The first songs Michael remembers singing were the Drifters' "Under the Boardwalk" and the

GROWING UP FAST
*Michael at the Jacksons'
Encino home in 1972:
"I'd like to be an actor,
like the kinds of things
Sidney Poitier does."*

Isley Brothers' "Twist and Shout." Today, onstage, Michael does a talk bit about how he feels the blues. It is not convincing; the Jackson 5 are not great actors just yet. But, with their median age still 15, they have paid dues.

The first show, Michael recalls, "was a hospital we did. They had a big Santa Claus." Another early show was at the Big Top; it was a shopping center. "We were doing it free so the people could hear the music. Before Motown," Michael says, "we used to do five shows a night for theaters" and clubs around Chicago and Gary, doing the circuit with groups like the Emotions and the Chi-Lites. The Jacksons also worked in Missouri and Wisconsin, and even in Arizona once. They got there by bus.

Now, seven years later, Michael is playing drums and learning the piano. And, in the Motown studios in Hollywood, backed

vocally by his brothers and instrumentally by the usual full crew of Motown session men, he sings lead. "It takes me about two hours to do one whole song," he says. "I do my part first, then they do theirs."

Mike is a skilled mimic. He watches TV cartoons and can sketch profiles; now he wants to take art in college. "Also I'd like to be an actor, like the kinds of things Sidney Poitier does." When I tell Michael he is a good blues singer, he laughs. "I learned by ear." And what about the screaming audiences? "If it weren't for the screaming, it wouldn't be exciting," he says. "The kids help us by being the way they are."

I F A J5 SHOW LACKS ANYTHING, IT'S SURPRISES. Whatever happens, you can tell it's been worked out in long rehearsal sessions at home in the Hollywood Hills or at Motown. Fans stand up, here and there, to their full four- or five-foot heights and scream; girls soul-slap with each other to celebrate eye contact with one of the Five; everywhere, kids are holding hands tightly in their excitement. But there is no mass movement, no jumping atop chairs and flooding of aisles, articulations of defiance, like at Sly concerts.

Later, at the Columbus airport, TWA gives the J5 entourage a special waiting room, saving them from a couple dozen autographs each – which is not to say they mind giving them. TWA brings in a tray of hamburgers and Cokes, and the J5 get down to chomping and arguing – mostly about the pillow fight the night before. "Suzanne, I saw you tripping someone last night," Michael says. "It was everybody against everybody."

After flying to their hometown of Gary, the J5 swing by City Hall, head to West Side High School for the day's first concert at 3 p.m., then to the mayor's home for a fairly private party. When the second show is finished they run out the back doors, pile into limousines and motor over to another section of Gary – for a Jackson family reunion at Joe Jackson's cousin's. She has worked a day and a half with friends and relatives to turn out two dozen sweet-potato pies, mountains of cold cuts and fried chicken, tubs of salad and black-eyed peas, and now she stands at the door, almost crying, so happy that her basement den is stuffed with people.

Joe and the boys are all here, along with some Commodores and just platoons of Jackson relations. They arrive, as if planned, in shifts, so that the aunts and cousins and sisters, beaming behind the food tables, stay busy serving all night. Joe's matronly cousin, damp-eyed, keeps asking if anybody wants more food. She steals a look or two at the Jackson 5, who eat lightly. Relatives and friends keep calling them away for a picture; little boys and girls ask for autographs, and the Jackson 5 do it all, graciously, saying, "Thank you," afterward. They're glad to be here. There's no place like home.

TABLE TALK
Fong-Torres, Tito, Randy, Marlon and Michael Jackson (from left) during a 1977 TV interview at Fong-Torres' San Francisco apartment, where Michael revisited his 1971 RS cover story. "He was smiling as he gazed at his cherubic image," Fong-Torres recalls.

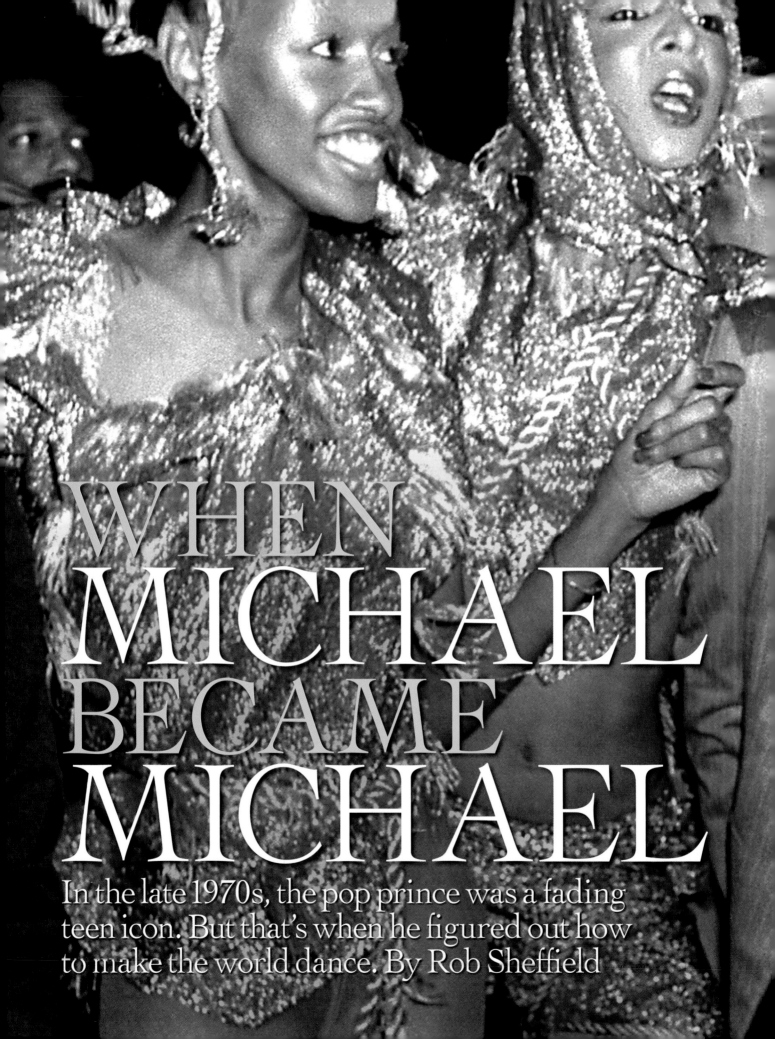

WHEN MICHAEL BECAME MICHAEL

In the late 1970s, the pop prince was a fading teen icon. But that's when he figured out how to make the world dance. By Rob Sheffield

THE JACKSONS' 1979 HIT "SHAKE YOUR BODY (DOWN TO THE GROUND)" BEGINS with a piano rumble, a cymbal glide, bass zooming from speaker to speaker. Tito Jackson tries out a staccato guitar lick. And then Michael Jackson lets loose the first whoops and gasps of his brand-new adult voice. See that girl over there? Michael can't tell if she notices him, if she recognizes him, if she even remembers he used to be in a big-deal kiddie group called the Jackson 5. All he knows is he needs to get close, so he slithers up to her on the dance floor with one of the all-time great disco opening lines: "I don't know what's gonna happen to you, baby, but I do! Know! That! I! Love ya!" ★ This song hit Number Seven in the spring of 1979, and it was more than the pivot point of MJ's career – in many ways,

it's the pivot point of pop music in the past 40 years. If there was a moment where Michael grew up and turned into Michael Jackson, this is it. On "Shake Your Body," he sounds totally confident – even though he was a very scared, emotionally ravaged, washed-up child star whose last big hit was years behind him – writing and producing his own material for the first time. He didn't know it, but he was just a year away from *Off the Wall*, the solo joint that made him the most beloved and desired creature in the pop universe.

The disco years are the only time Michael Jackson had anything close to a low profile – for the last time in his life, he was just another celebrity. By any standard, he was living a lush life of Hollywood fantasy: palling around with stars like Elizabeth Taylor and Liza Minnelli, playing the Scarecrow in *The Wiz* with Diana Ross, dating Tatum O'Neal, dancing at Studio 54. He was a strangely innocent boy-child in the era of *Boogie Nights* fleshpots, untouched by sex or drugs despite the manic indulgence all around him, a Jehovah's Witness lost in the pleasure dome. His private zoo grew like his collection of famous friends; he had to be the only virgin in Freddie Mercury's Rolodex. Everybody liked having this kid around. But nobody had any way of knowing that for him, this was just a warm-up.

The two Jacksons records that came out of this period, 1978's *Destiny* and 1980's *Triumph*, are disco classics that give a fascinating glimpse into MJ experimenting with his ideas in a family setting, inventing the sound that would explode in *Off the Wall* and *Thriller*. But they're also a document of his uneasy identity as a Jackson brother trapped in the family business, a megastar forced to keep pretending he's just another mem-

DRESS FOR SUCCESS
In 1977, Michael shows off a drum-major-like outfit that would presage his mid-1980s look. At right: Tito, Jackie, Michael, Jermaine and Marlon (from left) in Jamaica in 1975, the year they left Motown and went out on their own.

ber of the band, still living at home behind the iron gates of his father's compound.

By 1973, the hits had dried up for the Jackson 5, and the boys were given up for dead. Who wants yesterday's bubblegum? The comeback hit "Dancing Machine" – it reached Number Two in 1974 – must have seemed like a novelty fluke to the old guard at Motown, but it proved to be a prophetic hit. Disco was a new sound in 1974, and it was rare for a name R&B group to give up its major-artist prestige and go all out to reach the discothèque die-hards. "Dancing Machine" introduced the world to the Robot, which the Jacksons took all over the TV talk-show circuit, doing the dance with Cher and on *The Merv Griffin Show*.

The Jacksons left Motown for CBS Records in 1975, leaving their "5" behind, as Berry Gordy claimed it was his corporate property. The newly renamed Jacksons also left behind Jermaine, who'd married Gordy's daughter and stuck with Motown to start his solo career. With "Dancing Machine" as their exit strategy, the Jacksons seemed primed to become a fluffy pop family act like the Sylvers, the DeFranco Family or the Captain and Tennille. They went on *The Carol Burnett Show* to introduce their newest full-fledged member, Randy, the youngest Jackson brother and a burgeoning musical talent.

They made a pair of flops with the Philly-soul producers Gamble and Huff, who fed the brothers material while allowing Michael to write a couple of songs per album. *The Jacksons* has some moments – the Top 10 hit "Enjoy Yourself," the funk-rock "Think Happy," with its proto-"Beat It" guitar eruption, and Michael's solo songwriting debut, "Blues Away." But even the letter

MICHAEL MANIA
On the Jacksons' 1981 "Triumph" tour, Michael and his brothers played hits from "Off the Wall," released two years earlier.

'IN A WAY, 'OFF THE WALL' IS MY FAVORITE ALBUM, MORE THAN 'THRILLER,'" SAYS Quincy Jones, who produced both albums for Michael Jackson. "I just get a feel from it that it's got more range. We were just taking a lot of chances. We felt free." ★ *Off the Wall* propelled four singles into the Top 10 and established Jackson as the most important young black musical artist in America. It was eventually buried under the avalanche that was *Thriller,* but *Off the Wall* sold 20 million copies worldwide and broke the artistic ground that *Thriller* is built on. ★ *Off the Wall* is a dance album released at the height of disco fever, but it indulges in none of the genre's clichés. Its rhythms are smooth but propulsive, charged but gracefully syncopated; the melodies are light as air but immediate and unforgettable. Much of the credit for that sophistication goes to Jones, who assembled a

superb team of musicians and brought a deep understanding of jazz, orchestral music and other styles to the project. But Jackson's infectious demos for "Don't Stop 'Til You Get Enough" and "Working Day and Night" (which can be heard on the special 2001 edition of the album), both done with his brother Randy and sister Janet – who was 12 at the time – helping out on percussion, including glass bottles, demonstrate how conceptually realized those songs were when he presented them to Jones. Disappointed that some of his ideas had been left off the Jacksons' 1978 album *Destiny,* Michael was determined to make his next solo album outside the auspices of the family. "I didn't want *Off the Wall* to sound like outtakes from *Destiny,*" he later wrote. His brothers wanted desperately to work with him on the album, but Michael resisted (although Randy ended up playing percussion on "Don't Stop 'Til You Get Enough").

Jackson's domineering father gave his offhand blessings to the project, thinking that Michael just needed to get a solo album out of his system before returning to the family. "Go ahead, do what you want," Joe Jackson told Michael, "as long as it doesn't interfere with group business."

Michael Jackson and Quincy Jones had met in the early Seventies at a party at Sammy Davis Jr.'s house in Los Angeles. Jackson and Jones first worked together on the film *The Wiz* (1978), an African-American interpretation of *The Wizard of Oz* in which Jackson appeared as the Scarecrow. Jones, who served as the film's music supervisor, found in Jackson a refuge from what he regarded as the banality of much of the film's music.

"I saw a depth watching him when we did *The Wiz,*" Jones recalled in 2008. "He knew everybody's dialogue, he knew everybody's songs, he knew everybody's steps. I'd never seen somebody who could absorb so much so quickly."

Their connection solidified when Jones gently corrected Jackson's mispronunciation of a name in one of his lines. "It was 'Socrates,'" says Jackson's longtime engineer Bruce Swedien. "Michael pronounced it as 'So-*cray*-tees,' and Quincy straightened him out." Jackson had previously asked Jones if he could help him find a producer for the solo album he was about to begin working on. When he saw how warmly Jackson responded to his suggestion, Jones replied, "I'd like to take a shot at producing your new album."

It wasn't a likely pairing. For one thing, Jackson was barely out of his teens, and Jones was in his mid-40s. Jones had worked as an arranger and producer with the likes of Dizzy Gillespie, Frank Sinatra and Miles Davis, and Jackson's label, Epic, believed that he was "too jazzy." Only Jackson's insistence kept Jones – who had spent much of the 1970s working on film and TV scores – on the project.

Sessions for *Off the Wall* began in Los Angeles in December 1978 and lasted into the following spring. Rehearsals took place at Jones' house. "He was so shy, he'd sit down and sing behind the couch with his back to me, while I sat there with my hands over my eyes with the lights off," Jones wrote about Jackson in his 2001 autobiography, *Q.* Patti Austin, who duetted with Jackson on "It's the Falling in Love," describes her first encounter with Jackson: "It was like meeting a puppy – you put your hand out to them, then you let them come to you."

"We tried all kinds of things I'd learned over the years to help him with his artistic growth, like dropping keys just a minor third to give him flexibility and a more mature range in the upper and lower registers, and more than a few tempo changes," Jones said in his autobiography. "I also tried to steer him to songs with more depth, some of them about relationships. Seth Riggs, a leading vocal coach, gave him vigorous warm-up exercises to expand his top and bottom range by at least a fourth, which I desperately needed to get the vocal drama going." Jones also called in his A team of musicians, his "killer Q posse," including guitarists Larry Carlton and Motown's Wah Wah Watson. Jazz-fusion ace George Duke, future superstar producer David Foster, Toto's Steve Porcaro, and Greg Phillinganes, who was in Stevie Wonder's band and would become the musical director of Jackson's touring band, all played keyboards. Jones had recently produced hits for the funk group the Brothers Johnson, and he brought in "Get on the Floor," one of the band's unfinished studio tracks, which Jackson completed for the album.

MICHAEL'S MENTOR
Jackson and Jones in L.A. in 1979, the year "Off the Wall" made Jackson a solo superstar

The two dance-floor burners by Jackson – "Don't Stop 'Til You Get Enough" and "Working Day and Night" – were surrounded by tracks that had come in from all over. Although Wings had already recorded the song on their 1978 album *London Town,* Paul McCartney's ballad "Girlfriend" had been written with Jackson in mind, and Stevie Wonder contributed the swooning "I Can't Help It." Jones tapped Rod Temperton, who had written "Boogie Nights," a Number Two hit for his band Heatwave in 1977, to come up with some material for Jackson. Temperton wrote three songs, hoping Jackson and Jones would pick one. They took all three: "Off the Wall," "Rock With You" and "Burn This Disco Out."

Like Jones, Temperton did his best to play to Jackson's strengths. "I could tell from the melodies that Michael would sing on uptempo songs, he was very rhythmically driven," Temperton said. "So I tried to write melodies that had a lot of short notes, to give him some staccato rhythmic things he could do. The 'Off the Wall' title song gives you the best example [of that]."

Jackson did most of his vocals live, with no overdubs. "Michael's approach is very dramatic," Jones later said. "Very concise. When he commits to an idea, he goes all the way with it. . . . It's ass power, man. You have to be emotionally ready to put as much energy into it as it takes to make it right."

"The thing that I think was most impressive to me about Michael was his preparedness," says Swedien. "Michael would stay up all night the night before learning the lyrics so that he didn't have the lyrics in front of him when he recorded."

"Don't Stop 'Til You Get Enough" opens the album with a sexy, uptempo surge, as well as a bold declaration of Jackson's ambitions. The song's sensuality ("I'm melting/Like hot candle wax") was itself a departure for Jackson, an undeniable message that the young boy who had charmed millions with the Jackson 5 had grown up and become a man. When Michael played the song for his mother, Katherine, she wondered if the title contained a sexual reference. "Well, if you think it means something dirty, then that's what it'll mean," he told her. "But that's not how I intended it."

GROWING UP IN PUBLIC
"Off the Wall" was released the same month (August 1979) Michael turned 21.

But the Jacksons had already had their share of dance hits, and, like Jones, Jackson felt that *Off the Wall* needed something more. "The ballads were what made *Off the Wall* a Michael Jackson album," Jackson later said. "I'd done ballads with [my] brothers, but they had never been too enthusiastic about them and did them more as a concession to me than anything else." Jones had been saving "She's Out of My Life" for Sinatra but ended up offering it to Jackson. (The song, by Tom Bahler, was reportedly written about his breakup with Karen Carpenter of the soft-pop duo the Carpenters.) "That's from a real-life experience, a very emotional song. And you've got to remember, when I first saw Michael on the Academy Awards, he was singing a love song to a rat!" Jones said, recalling Jackson's 1972 hit "Ben." Jackson broke down crying every time he sang "She's Out

of My Life" in the studio. Finally Jones decided to include the parts where Jackson's voice cracks on the album.

"I knew it was an experience he'd never even thought about. . . . It's a very mature emotion," said Jones of the heartbreak in the song and of the surprising depth of Jackson's rendering of it. "I didn't know how he was relating to it. He'd never had that kind of mature relationship with anybody, I don't think."

A few weeks after *Off the Wall*'s release, Michael celebrated his 21st birthday at Studio 54. He seemed entirely in tune with the times, coming of age at the epicenter of the urban-nightlife scene sweeping the culture, and creating a smart, sexy soundtrack for it. Even *Off the Wall*'s cover carried unmistakable meaning. Rather than sporting a stage get-up, Jackson is wearing a sharp tuxedo, a grown-up look that could be from a photo taken at a graduation or wedding, or any other significant rite of passage. (To offset the tux's seriousness, Jackson insisted on wearing spangled socks.)

More significantly, Jackson is still wearing his hair in a modified Afro – he's identifiably black and seems perfectly at ease being so. Jackson came to believe that his blackness had limited the recognition that *Off the Wall* received. Given the album's popularity and critical standing, Jackson reasonably anticipated that it would get a number of Grammy nominations, including one for Album of the Year. Instead, the album was not nominated in any of the three major categories for which it was eligible and won only one Grammy: Best Male R&B Vocal

MOUNTAIN HIGH
Jackson in the Alps in Switzerland in 1979, during a break in the "Off the Wall" sessions

Performance, for "Don't Stop 'Til You Get Enough." Jackson felt that the music industry was trying to keep him in his place as a niche artist: a black singer making dance music.

"You have to keep in mind what happened to Michael during the 1980 Grammy Awards. . . . ," a member of Jackson's camp told ROLLING STONE in 1988. "That experience hurt Michael, and it also taught him a lesson. You could be the biggest black entertainer in history, and yet to much of the music industry and media, you were an invisible man." Jackson regarded the snub as "totally unfair" and insisted that it could "never happen again."

And it wouldn't. Jackson and Jones went on a mission, and *Thriller*'s crossover moves were executed with the precision of a military campaign. The rise of MTV, where Jackson had other barricades to crack, made the visual and performance aspects of Jackson's appeal readily available at virtually all times to a young audience that the music business desperately needed. His genius could no longer be denied.

Still, in gaining those lost Grammys and incalculable commercial success, Jackson perhaps lost something greater. *Off the Wall* embodies an ease and relaxed confidence that you find less and less often in his later music, however great and important much of it is. The joyous urgency of "Don't Stop 'Til You Get Enough" would eventually yield to the fear that, for Jackson, no amount of acclaim, recognition or success ever really would be enough.

DANCING MACHINE

Michael's moves changed the pop landscape and even impressed legends like Astaire. By Douglas Wolk

A NY SHORTLIST OF THE GREATEST AND MOST INFLUENTIAL MALE DANCERS of the 20th century – Fred Astaire, Mikhail Baryshnikov, Bill "Bojangles" Robinson – would have to include Michael Jackson. "He was a formidable dancer – he knew what was really right for him," says Baryshnikov. "His dance was fluid and very dominant. He had maybe 10 moves, but he'd paint these moves for different purposes – to be sexy, to shock." ★ "What Michael brought to the dance world was taking a vocabulary that was a synthesis of the classic movement of Fred Astaire, some of Jackie Wilson, some of James Brown and street movement, and putting them together into a new style that had never been seen before," says Broadway choreographer Vincent Paterson, who worked with Jackson for 17 years. Jackson was never formally trained as

a dancer, but he was a student of dance his entire life, picking up ideas wherever he could find them. He soaked up moves from *Soul Train*, from mime, from street dance, from Bob Fosse.

As far back as his early childhood, Jackson remembered watching James Brown on TV. "I'd get angry at the cameraman, because whenever he would really start to dance they would be on a close-up, so I couldn't see his feet," he said in 1993. "I'd shout, 'Show him! Show him!' so I could watch and learn."

By his teens, Jackson was already a hugely influential dancer. He didn't invent the Robot, but within a few days of his 1973 "Dancing Machine" performance on *Soul Train*, "it seemed that every kid in the United States was doing the Robot," Jackson wrote in his autobiography. Jackson, who had a lifelong obsession with the golden age of Hollywood, idolized Fred Astaire. "When we were making the 'Smooth Criminal' video, he had us watch [Astaire's 1953 movie] *The Band Wagon*, and we based it off of that," says Eddie Garcia, who danced with Jackson on the *Bad* and *Dangerous* tours. "We all had different gangsters to watch: 'You're *that* guy, you're *that* guy.'"

By the time Jackson's solo career began in earnest with *Off the Wall*, he'd become a world-class dancer. "What you want in

dance is rhythmic quality," says *The New Yorker*'s dance critic, Joan Acocella, "but you also need clarity. He had immense clarity. If you look at 'Don't Stop 'Til You Get Enough,' he doesn't have the absolutely fine edge that you get later in 'Billie Jean,' but you see the relaxation, the charm, the utter commitment to the dance."

"He was truly innocent about other forms of dance," says Baryshnikov. "He and Liz Taylor came to see me dance in L.A. with White Oak and at the Shrine Auditorium. He was a curious man – he knew very little about ballet or modern dance, but he asked about how I work with choreographers. I explained to him how Mark Morris or Twyla Tharp were the creators of the work and I was their vessel. He was surprised that I had very little to say about my work. Liz Taylor said it was likely the first time he had ever seen ballet."

Jackson's crowning glory as a dancer came during his performance of "Billie Jean" on the Motown 25th-anniversary TV special in 1983 – when he astonished the massive television audience with the physics-defying backward stroll that he dubbed

SMOOTH MOVES
Jackson at the 1995 MTV Video Music Awards. His "Scream" video won an award for best choreography.

DANCING KINGS
Jackson and James Brown (above) at the BET
Awards in 2003. As a kid, Jackson picked up moves
from watching Brown on TV. Opposite page: the
Jackson 5 on "The Ed Sullivan Show" in 1970.

the "moonwalk." Fred Astaire called Jackson the day after the special and told him, "You're a hell of a mover." "That was the greatest compliment I had ever received in my life, and the only one I had ever wanted to believe," Jackson later said. Naturally, a lot of people would like to take credit for inventing the moonwalk – or at least teaching it to Jackson.

One likely genealogy involves Jeffrey Daniel, a member of Shalamar who'd pulled off a remarkable moonwalk on British TV in 1982 and worked with Jackson on some *Bad*-era videos. Jackson himself said he picked the moonwalk up from watching "kids dancing on the street": "I took a mental picture of it, a mental movie of it. I went into my room upstairs in Encino [California], and I would just start doing the dance and create and perfect it." Says Paterson, "He would invite street kids to come in and work with him, to teach him what was going on in the streets."

Jackson created a near-universal style and aesthetic for dancing in pop-music videos – adopted by everyone from Madonna to Miley Cyrus. "It was through his videos that dancers became an essential part of music video," says Garcia. "Between 'Beat It' and 'Thriller,' he set the standard that everyone tries to live up to." Adds Paterson, "And before Michael, there was a huge stigma about guys dancing. Michael destroyed that stigma."

In his later years, Jackson remained able to command attention by dancing without any music at all. At the beginning of each show on the 1992-93 *Dangerous* tour, he would suddenly appear onstage, and stand there, motionless, for a few minutes,

with the audience roaring at the simple manifestation of his body. "It's a sign of masterfulness as a dancer to stop moving," says dance critic Apollinaire Scherr. "He was always doing that – even when he was a boy, he'd do something where he'd just move his heel or his toes, and everything else would be still. That's what makes him so hip: He's not in any hurry."

Still, Jackson tended to repeat a handful of favorite tricks – the abrupt shoulder-pops, the pencil turns, the thrust-out left leg, the crotch-grabs and pelvic thrusts that seemed more harmless the more he repeated them. That was the problem with his dancing in his later years, Scherr argues, "At a certain point, he became a brand," forced to reprise his signature gestures until they went stale. Acocella concurs, "Sometimes he was wasteful of his powers as a dancer."

But his influence on dance continued long after he'd all but stopped performing. As Antonio "LA" Reid said, "You can see his influence in his sister Janet, in Justin Timberlake, Usher and Britney Spears, in the syncopated choreography that a lot of young artists use." Kenny Ortega, the director of what would have been Jackson's This Is It concerts, recalls that "over 5,600 dancers applied, from all over the world, to audition. All of them were there because Michael was their sole inspiration. One of the dancers was asked, 'Now that you're dancing with Michael Jackson, what next?' And he said, 'I don't know! I can't conceive of it, because this was all I ever dreamed of. The goal in my life was to be able to dance with Michael Jackson!'"

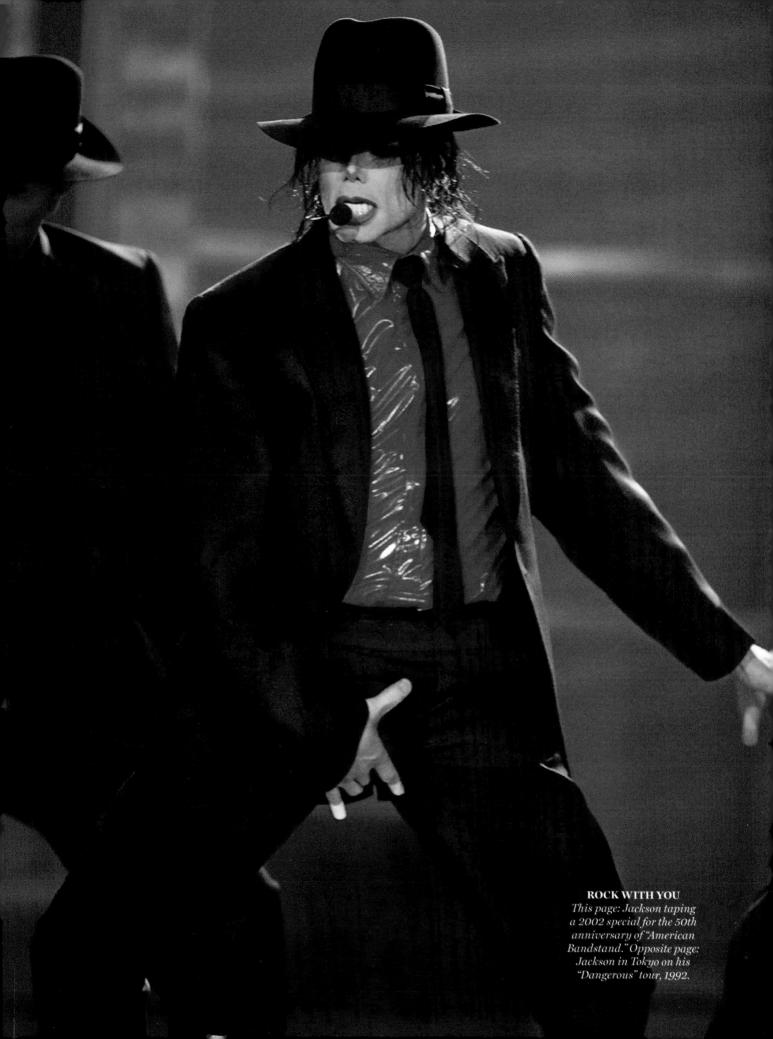

ROCK WITH YOU
This page: Jackson taping a 2002 special for the 50th anniversary of "American Bandstand." Opposite page: Jackson in Tokyo on his "Dangerous" tour, 1992.

STARTIN' SOMETHIN'
*Jackson debuted his gravity-
defying lean in the 1988
"Smooth Criminal" video.*

MAN IN THE MIRROR
Jackson in a Neverland Ranch studio in 1991

ON TOP OF THE WORLD

How Michael Jackson and Quincy Jones made
the bestselling album of all time. By Alan Light

MAYBE IT WAS A SIGN WHEN THE speakers in the studio burst into flames. It was late October 1982, and a full battalion of musicians and technicians were working around the clock at Westlake Recording Studios in Los Angeles, putting the finishing touches on Michael Jackson's new album. The disc was the highly anticipated follow-up to 1979's *Off the Wall*, which had established him as a solo superstar. In fact, the first single from the new disc had already been released – "The Girl Is Mine," a winsome duet with Paul McCartney – adding pressure to wrap things up quickly. And the song Jackson and crew were completing would prove to be the album's most ambitious, radical achievement, the cut that ended up breaking the project wide open.

"When we were finishing 'Beat It,' we had three studios going," recalls Quincy Jones, who was producing the sessions. "We had Eddie Van Halen in one; Michael was in another, singing a part through a cardboard tube; and we were mixing in another. We were working five nights and five days, with no sleep. And at one point, the speakers overloaded and caught on fire!"

One month later, *Thriller* was released, and pop music would never be the same again. The album reached Number One in February 1983, stayed atop the charts for a record-shattering 37 weeks and has sold more than an estimated 50 million copies worldwide. In today's world of declining sales and fragmented audiences, it is almost impossible to imagine how much this one album dominated and united the culture.

When asked today about *Thriller*, Jones points out – taking care to insist that he is not minimizing Jackson's role – that it requires an entire brain trust to make a classic album. "Michael didn't create *Thriller*," he says. "It takes a team to make an album. He wrote four songs, and he sang his ass off, but he didn't conceive it – that's not how an album works." Jones gives particular credit to the contributions of engineer Bruce Swedien and of songwriter Rod Temperton, who had written the hits "Always and Forever" and "Boogie Nights" as a member of the multiracial R&B group Heatwave. He had become a trusted Jones collaborator, contributing three songs for *Off the Wall*, including "Rock With You" and the title track.

Michael had started working on *Thriller* in the recording studio at the Jacksons' home in Encino, California, in the days following the breakthrough of *Off the Wall*, which firmly established him as a major pop icon. He was determined, unwaveringly focused on the idea that he would create not just something to equal or even surpass *Off the Wall*, but an album on which every one of the songs would be a hit single.

PERFECT HARMONY
When the "Victory" tour stopped in Dallas in July 1984, Eddie Van Halen made a surprise appearance and re-created his "Beat It" solo.

GOT TO BE THERE
Michael and the Jacksons onstage at New York's Madison Square Garden in August 1984

Until *Off the Wall*, Jackson had struggled with songwriting. Now, he found it coming easier, as he told ROLLING STONE's Gerri Hirshey. "I wake up from dreams and go, 'Wow, put this down on paper,'" he said in 1982. The Jackson composition that formally kicked off the recording of *Thriller* (cited, in the notes to the 2001 "Special Edition" reissue of the album, as commencing on Wednesday, April 14th, 1982, at noon) was "The Girl Is Mine," in which Jackson shared the vocals with Paul McCartney.

First, Jackson and Jones visited McCartney at his ranch in Tucson, Arizona, spending a couple of days rehearsing and indulging in the musicians' shared obsession with cartoons. "When I approached Paul," Jackson wrote in his 1988 book *Moonwalk*, "I wanted to repay the favor he had done me in contributing 'Girlfriend' to *Off the Wall*."

McCartney, however, expressed some trepidation about the song's bubblegum feel. He was especially concerned about the cloying use of the word "doggone." "You could say it's shallow," he admitted. "When I checked it out with Michael, he explained that he wasn't going for depth, he was going for rhythm, he was going for feel."

Toto guitarist Steve Lukather, who had gotten a call from Jackson himself to play on several of *Thriller*'s songs (and cursed the singer out and hung up on him several times, convinced it was a prank), played on "The Girl Is Mine." "The McCartney duet was really insane," he says. "You can imagine what kind of a zoo it was, with Michael and Quincy and McCartney and all the people and the staff and the security. We never even got into the control room – [Beatles producer] George Martin and [Beatles engineer] Geoff Emerick were there, Dick Clark. It was so intense."

Though far from *Thriller*'s finest moment, "The Girl Is Mine" has a breezy charm, and Jackson instantly knew his plans for the song, calling it "the obvious first single." In *Moonwalk*, he wrote that "we really didn't have much choice. When you have two strong names like that together on a song, it has to come out first or it gets played to death and overexposed. We had to get it out of the way."

To Jackson's record company, the song represented a chance to start thinking about a global strategy for *Thriller* that would prove historic. "We tried to take a worldwide view of Michael," said Don Dempsey, then-senior vice president of Epic Records, in 1984. "We were seeing some initial interest in Michael outside the U.S., and we felt that one of the ways to really propel that was the duet with Paul McCartney." (Still, Quincy Jones notes that there was some resistance to the interracial romance implied by the song. "Radio didn't like the idea of Paul and Michael fighting over the same girl, and some stations wouldn't play it," he says.)

Jackson's instincts proved correct – the song made it to Number Two on the pop charts and Number One on the R&B singles chart. Not only was it the first time a Beatle topped the R&B list, but the song that it knocked out of that slot was "Sexual Healing," the comeback smash by Jackson's old Motown labelmate Marvin Gaye.

As "The Girl Is Mine" headed into the marketplace, Jackson continued recording for the album. He and Jones listened to hundreds of songs, trying to find the range and balance that would create the album he was dreaming of. He cut "Wanna Be Startin' Somethin'," a song he reportedly started writing during the *Off the Wall* period. Its chattering groove and swirling arrangement are the closest thing on *Thriller* to the previous album, which may be one reason it was chosen as the opening track. But there was a new tone in Jackson's lyrics, an edge of fear and paranoia ("You're a vegetable/Still they hate you. . . . You're just a buffet . . . they eat off of you").

The song's other memorable feature was an African chant in the concluding section, a slight variation on Cameroonian saxophonist Manu Dibango's 1972 proto-disco hit "Soul Makossa." "Michael heard that, and he liked it," says Jones. "I said, 'Michael, that's Manu Dibango's record,' and he said, 'But I need it!'" (Dibango was not given a songwriting credit, but a financial settlement was eventually reached.)

Among the other songs cut during the early phases of the *Thriller* sessions were Rod Temperton's loose, swinging "Baby Be Mine" (which, Jones points out, has a melody similar to a John Coltrane-style progressive jazz line) and another Temperton song that began life under the innocuous title "Starlight." Somewhere along the line, he picked up on Jackson's love of horror movies, and gave the lyrics a more ominous feel. "Starlight" became "Thriller" and was given a theatrical, dramatic arrangement. The song found a balance between a Broadway-style narrative and a thumping, irresistible dance-floor beat. "I had always envisioned a talking section at the end," Temperton said in an interview included on the CD reissue of *Thriller*, "but I didn't really know what to do with it."

YOU ARE NOT ALONE
Jackson greets London fans after the 1985 unveiling of his wax likeness at Madame Tussauds.

It turned out that Jones' then-wife, Peggy Lipton, knew the legendary horror-movie actor Vincent Price. "The idea was that he would just talk some horror talk like he would deliver in his famous roles," said Temperton. "The night before the session, Quincy called and said, 'I'm a bit scared. Perhaps you better write something for him.'" Temperton wrote one verse of the groovy ghoulish rap that closes the song while waiting for a taxi to the studio and then two more verses during the ride. "Rod wrote this brilliant Edgar Allan Poe spiel," said Jones. "And Vincent really understood it. . . . Vincent did it in two takes."

Lukather recalls Jackson's intensity during the album's creation. "Michael was very focused, he knew what he wanted," he says. "When he'd start dancing to a groove, that's when we knew we were playing the right shit. He wasn't, like, moonwalking across the room, but the hands and feet were going, he and Quincy were bopping. That would create a whole other vibe, and you'd really want to kill it. It was a great working environment."

The most hotly debated song from the first half of *Thriller*'s sessions would prove to be the album's central track. As the demo included on the 2001 reissue reveals, Jackson had a very clear sense

VICTORY IS MINE
Michael at Dodger Stadium during the closing stand of the "Victory" tour, December 1984. "I didn't want to go on the 'Victory' tour, and I fought against it," Michael wrote in "Moonwalk." "But my brothers wanted to do it, and I did it for them. It was a nice feeling, playing with my brothers again."

of the sound and the groove for "Billie Jean" – one of the four songs he contributed to the album – from the beginning. But Jones contended that the instrumental introduction was too long. "You could shave on that intro," said Jones. "But he said, 'That's the jelly, that's what makes me want to dance.' And when Michael Jackson tells you that's what makes him want to dance, well, the rest of us just have to shut up."

Drummer N'dugu Chancler was brought in to give extra propulsion to an already massive beat. "Michael always knew how he wanted it to sound," Chancler once said. "There was originally just a drum-machine track on it. I came in and cut a live-drum track over the overdub." To add another layer of "ear candy," jazzman Tom Scott plays an uncredited solo on an obscure horn called a lyricon that is woven throughout the song.

Then there were the lyrics. "Billie Jean" told a chilling tale of being falsely accused and living in terror, a caution to "be careful of what you do, 'cause the lie becomes the truth." These were emotions no one had ever heard before from the former boy wonder. "I figured that he was making a conscious effort . . . to change his image," wrote Michael's mother, Katherine, in her book, *My Family, The Jacksons*. "I think he felt that his image had become too goody-goody."

REALLY, THOUGH, THE SONG'S STORY WAS based in fact – though Jackson never revealed that to his closest collaborators, not even Quincy Jones. When Gerri Hirshey of ROLLING STONE noticed a snapshot tucked into a picture frame in Jackson's dining room, Jackson acknowledged that she was the real Billie Jean; Hirshey described her as "a black teenager of average countenance, posing, most likely, for a high school yearbook." Jackson explained that she had written him, claiming that he had fathered her child, and sent him a weapon with instructions about when and how he should kill himself. "I want to memorize her face," he explained, "in case she ever does turn up someplace."

ON YOUR TOES
On the "Victory" tour, which usually kicked off each night with "Wanna Be Startin' Somethin'"

In *Moonwalk*, Jackson changed his account, presumably to discourage any future psychopaths. "There never was a real Billie Jean," he wrote. "The girl in the song is a composite of people we've been plagued by over the years." Even as late as 2001, Jones said the song's subject was "a girl who climbed over the wall . . . and invaded the place. . . . She accused him of being the father of one of her twins!" The final hurdle was convincing Jones to stick with Jackson's title for the song. It was almost released as "Not My Lover," because the producer was concerned that people would think it was a song about tennis player Billie Jean King.

With "Billie Jean" wrapped, Jackson and Jones had nine songs in the can. "When we got down to nine," says Jones, "we put those on their feet to see if they stood up. I tried to be as objective as I could and take the four weakest out of those nine and replace them. They weren't weak, it was great stuff, but you have to be realistic."

"There was a point we thought it was all over, that we were all finished," remembers *Thriller* keyboard player Greg Phillinganes. "There had been so much hard work and long hours, and Quincy's saying, 'It's not there yet,' and Michael, almost distraught, is saying, 'What are we going to do now?'" One of the songs that got knocked out was a light, lyrical song called "Carousel," which eventually saw the light of day on the 2001 *Thriller* rerelease. But another song had presented itself that had the same sort of mood.

"Toto [some of whose members appear on much of *Thriller*] sent over two demos," said Jones. "They were OK, but we left the tape running, and at the end was all this silence, then there was this dummy lyric, a very skeletal thing . . . but such a wonderful flavor." Jones sent the demo to a writer named John Bettis, who responded with a lyric titled "Human Nature." As the song developed, Lukather added "all these weird, metered hooky parts," earning an arranging credit. Jackson gave a breathy, lighter-than-air performance, resulting in *Thriller*'s most memorable pure-pop moment. "Human Nature" would also become a staple of jazz giant Miles Davis' live set during the trumpeter's later years.

The final additions to the *Thriller* lineup revealed the tactical thinking of Jackson and Jones. The singer was setting out to make the biggest album in history. As Jones would put it, "To penetrate, you have to go for the throat in four, five, six different areas: rock, AC, R&B, soul."

Temperton's "The Lady in My Life," a classic Sinatra-style ballad, would close the album, providing the final grace note. "P.Y.T. (Pretty Young Thing)" – named after a brand of lingerie Jones' wife liked – was the only track on *Thriller* on which the producer was credited as a songwriter, alongside soul balladeer James Ingram. It was the album's closest thing to straight-up contemporary R&B, with a flirty Jackson vocal over some chirping synthesizers and slightly embarrassing Eighties slang (would Michael Jackson ever really say "to the max" or call a girl a "tenderoni"?). "It was just another groove," says Jones. "I've been playing those kind of grooves since I was with Ray Charles."

But there was still one final card left to play. "I had been thinking I wanted to write the type of rock song that I would go out and buy," Jackson wrote. Jones said back in 1984 that "we were very conscious of wanting a white rock & roll groove. And when Smelly [his nickname for Jackson, after the word the polite-to-a-fault singer used when he was too embarrassed to describe a song as "funky"] wrote 'Beat It,' we knew he'd come up with the nitroglycerin." Later, the producer would say that he felt the album had needed "a song like 'My Sharona,' a black version of a strong rock & roll thing."

"Beat It" was, like its companion song, "Billie Jean," evidence of the growth in Jackson's songwriting. Its words are a condemnation of violence that isn't simple-minded or preachy. And the groove was a killer, with a convincing and unforced rock flavor. To guide the rhythm section, Jackson pounded on boxes in the studio (he's listed in the credits as "drum-case beater"). But it was Jones who had the inspired idea to bring in reigning guitar god Eddie Van Halen. It helped that Jackson was friendly with Van Halen's then-wife, actress Valerie Bertinelli. Much like Lukather, though, Van Halen hung up on Jones several times before he could be convinced that it really was the legendary producer asking for help. The guitarist quickly came on board and even refused payment for the session: "I did it as a favor," he said.

When Van Halen came in to record his solo, Jones told him, "I'm not gonna sit here and try to tell you what to play – the reason you're here is 'cause of what you do play." When Lukather heard that Van Halen was going to add the solo, he decided to really kick out the jams. "When they told me Eddie was playing on it, and they were trying to do a crossover record, I whipped out the Marshalls and did a wall of fucking sound," he says. "Quincy sent that back and said, 'The guitars are too heavy, they'll never play this on R&B radio,' so I went down to little Fenders and just did it again."

Even so, the sound of "Beat It" was simply outrageous, for both rock and R&B listeners. Island Def Jam chairman LA Reid remembers being blown away. "Today we do things called 'mash-ups,' right?" he says. "Take Linkin Park and Jay-Z and put it together, and it's certainly unique, but it's not unusual. But at that time, Eddie Van Halen was at the top of his game and fit right in with 'Beat It.' It didn't feel like a guitar solo over some R&B track. It was very organic. The idea of it was really unusual, but the results weren't strained at all."

VICTORY DANCE
After winning eight Grammys for "Thriller," Jackson went out on the road with his brothers.

The overdubs on "Beat It" were the last parts recorded for *Thriller.* The team worked until 9 a.m. Bruce Swedien took the tapes to be mastered, and Quincy Jones took Michael Jackson back to his house. "I put him on the couch and pulled a blanket over him," he says, "and then we had to go back at noon to listen to the master."

Unfortunately, this late in the game, the album didn't have the punch they were hoping for. It was too long to fit on a standard LP, for one thing, requiring thin grooves that produced tinny sound. They decided to cut a verse from "The Lady in My Life" and shorten that contested introduction on "Billie Jean." Then, as the clock continued to tick, they opted to remix the entire album (except for "The Girl Is Mine," which was already all over the radio), one track a day for eight days. The final day of mixing was Monday, November 8th, 1982. Twenty-two days later, *Thriller* was available in stores. Michael Jackson was 24 years old.

The amazing thing, claimed Gerri Hirshey in 1985, was that "Michael had predicted it all when I first met him – the media geek show, the staggering sales figures, the order of singles, the fact that 'Billie Jean' would be the breakout song."

"You can't explain something like that," Jones says. "It's why I used to keep a sign in the studio saying, 'Always leave space for God to walk into the room.'"

But there is one thing he is sure of: "When a record goes to Number One," says Jones, "everything starts with the songs."

ON TOP OF THE WORLD
Michael in New York, February 7th, 1984. That week, "Thriller" became the seventh Top 40 hit from the album of the same name.

USA AFRICA
United Support of Artists for Africa

MICHAEL
GIVES BACK

Jackson and his friends sang for Africa
and made history along the way

STAR POWER
First row, from left: Paul Simon, Kim Carnes, Michael Jackson, Diana Ross, Stevie Wonder, Quincy Jones. Second row, from left: Billy Joel, Cyndi Lauper, Bruce Springsteen, Willie Nelson, James Ingram, Bob Dylan. Third row, from left: Daryl Hall, Dionne Warwick, Al Jarreau, Kenny Rogers, Huey Lewis. John Oates, Johnny Colla. Back row, from left: Lionel Richie, Steve Perry, Kenny Loggins, Jeffrey Osborne, Lindsey Buckingham, Dan Aykroyd, Harry Belafonte, Bob Geldof.

When Michael Jackson and Lionel Richie wrote "We Are the World" in early 1985, they were the two biggest musical acts in the world. They had been friends since the Commodores opened for the Jackson 5 back in 1971, but they had never actually collaborated on anything before. "We spent a day at his house listening to everything from 'The Star-Spangled Banner' to 'God Save the Queen' to figure out the majestic quality," says Richie. "From there we kind of doodled and hummed the song out, and Michael took those doodles and went with a keyboard player and sung the melody with someone playing behind him. And there lies the song."

The idea of creating an all-star charity single originated with Bob Geldof, who months earlier had spearheaded Band Aid's "Do They Know It's Christmas?" in the U.K. to raise money for drought-ravaged Ethiopia. Weeks after that song exploded on the British charts, Richie and Jackson began work on America's response. Recruiting musicians proved to be easy, especially once Bruce Springsteen – then at the height of his fame – signed on to the project. Studio time was booked at Hollywood's A&M Studios on January 28th, 1985 – the night of the American Music Awards, which guaranteed that the majority of the artists would be in town. Jackson skipped the awards so he could cut a guide vocal for the artists with producer Quincy Jones. Around 10 p.m., a fleet of limos began pulling up to the studio, and in walked Bob Dylan, Paul Simon, Diana Ross, Tina Turner, Cyndi Lauper, Billy Joel, Ray Charles, Stevie Wonder and 36 others. Jones placed a sign at the entrance stating "Check Your Egos at the Door."

One invited artist who never showed up was Prince (a spot on the floor next to Michael Jackson was marked with a piece of tape that read "Prince"). Although he called late in the session offering to add a guitar part, it was vocals that were required, so Prince never made it. "He didn't come – why not?" steamed Geldof. "That's the question. Has he got other things that are more important than trying to save people's lives? Going to a disco?"

Otherwise, the 10-hour session was remarkably smooth. With Jones conducting the singers and Richie and Jackson molding the music, the choir spent its first few hours on singing the chorus along with the prerecorded backing track and stacking harmonies on top of it. After that, individual singers were assigned snippets of verse. There were also some brief duets: Jackson and Ross, Lauper and Huey Lewis, Joel and Turner. ("It was only four words," said an elated Joel, "but as far as I'm concerned, I did a duet with Tina Turner!")

At one point during recording, Wonder adopted Dylan's characteristic nasal bray to show Dylan how to sing a part; at another, Geldof and Dan Aykroyd duetted on some R&B oldies, including "Barefootin'" and "Walking the Dog." Smokey Robinson broke into a spontaneous rendition of Harry Belafonte's Fifties hit "Banana Boat (Day-O)," and soon the whole group was chiming in for an extended version of the song – prompting friends and managers secluded on a nearby sound-stage (stocked with buffet eats and drinks and big video screens to monitor the artists-only studio session) to exclaim, "This should be the B side!" For a while, Wonder was determined to inject some actual Ethiopian lyrics into the song's choruses – "It's got to be authentic!" he said – and he dispatched various aides to determine the correct words. But Charles noted that they were having enough trouble singing the song in English, and in the end Wonder's plan fell through.

Certain stars seemed somewhat cowed by all the talent in the room: Dylan and Springsteen were strangely subdued (although Springsteen later "really got into it," according to one onlooker), and the ever-shy Jackson was not observed making eye contact with anyone all evening. Quincy Jones called the session the high point of his 35-year career. "Nothing else surpasses it," he said. "Conducting that choir – I had goose bumps. And the goose bumps were up all night long. It was unbelievable. Some powerful energy."

The evening's occasional breaks were almost as animated as the long stretches of recording. Bette Midler took one such opportunity to end a long-running feud with Paul Simon ("We've been small-mouthing each other for years, but it was such a warm occasion, we sort of buried the hatchet") and got down to a cackle-stoked chat with Ruth Pointer about various old boyfriends they had in common. Ross broke the ice by taking around her sheet music for autographs, and soon everybody was at it. Springsteen solicited Steve Perry's autograph for a friend's daughter, and Perry asked the same of Jackson for one of his friends' sons. Dylan, whose first session job had been playing harmonica on a 1961 Harry Belafonte version of "Midnight Special" (a tedious experience, according to the Dylan legend), must have mellowed toward the memory – in autographing Belafonte's music sheet, he wrote, "Thanks for giving me my start."

After the "We Are the World" single was released on March 7th, 1985, it shot to Number One. By mid-May, USA for Africa had raised $6.5 million. "It was like Magic Johnson, Michael Jordan and Kobe Bryant playing a game of pickup," Richie says now. "We were all so on our game at that point, we could've coughed and made it work."

At the 1986 Grammys, "We Are the World" won four awards – including Record of the Year and Song of the Year. "I'm going to be presumptuous enough to speak for this great group," Jones said that night. "I'd like to thank them and apologize that the slogan 'keep your egos at the door' ever got out of hand, because it was never necessary. . . .This generation changed from I, me, mine to we, you, us."

Jackson shared the sentiment. "First I'd like to thank God," he said. "And I'd like to say thank you for choosing Lionel and myself to write 'We Are the World.' I'd like to thank Quincy Jones, who is the greatest producer to me. . . . When you leave here, remember the children."

Compiled from original Rolling Stone *reports by Kurt Loder and Michael Goldberg in RS 443 (March 14, 1985) and RS 444 (March 28, 1985), with additional reporting by Andy Greene.*

INSIDE THE MAGICAL KINGDOM

In 1982, Michael Jackson sat down at home –
unguarded and unmasked – for a lengthy
interview and a petting session with his snake
By Gerri Hirshey

RS 389 · FEBRUARY 17, 1983

In the fall of 1982, just as Michael Jackson was releasing *Thriller*, he invited ROLLING STONE correspondent Gerri Hirshey into his rented condo in the San Fernando Valley for what would be his last-ever in-depth print interview. By this time, Jackson was intensely private and isolated, fearful of how he would be presented by the media. But when Hirshey showed up, Jackson answered the door himself, dressed in dirty corduroys and scuffed oxfords. There were no managers or family members with him, and Hirshey says he was a "touchingly inept" host; when the lemonade she was drinking ran out, he filled her glass with warm Hawaiian Punch. Over the course of several days, Hirshey interviewed Jackson at home, accompanied him to the studio and even tagged along with him to a Queen concert. She came away with a first-hand look at Jackson's isolation and eccentricity. At one point, Jackson asked Hirshey to hold his eight-foot boa constrictor, Muscles. "He explained it was an exercise in trust, and he was most convincing," she says. "If I was scared of snakes, he had a mortal dread of reporters."

MICHAEL

IT'S NOON, AND SOMEWHERE IN THE SAN FERN-ando Valley, the front shades of a row of condos are lowered against a hazy glare. All along the courtyard's trimmed inner paths, poodles waddle about trailing poodle-cut ladies on pink leashes.

"Not what you expected, huh?" From behind a mask of bony fingers, Michael Jackson giggles. Having settled his visitor on the middle floor of his own three-level condo, Michael explains that the residence is temporary, while his Encino, California, home is razed and rebuilt. He concedes that this is an unlikely spot for a young prince of pop.

It is also surprising to see that Michael has decided to face this interview alone. He says he has not done anything like this for over two years. And even when he did, it was always with a cordon of managers, other Jackson brothers and, in one case, his younger sister, Janet, parroting a reporter's questions before Michael would answer them. The small body of existing literature paints him as excruciatingly shy. He ducks, he hides, he talks to his shoe tops. Or he just doesn't show up. He is known to conduct his private life with almost obsessive caution, "just like a hemophiliac who can't afford to be scratched in any way." The analogy is his.

Run this down next to the stats, the successes, and it doesn't add up. He has been the featured player with the Jackson 5 since grade school. In 1979, he stepped out of the Jacksons to release his own LP, *Off the Wall,* and it was certified platinum by the end of the year. *Thriller,* his new album, is Number Five on the charts. And the list of performers now working with him – or wanting to – includes Paul McCartney, Quincy Jones, Steven Spielberg, Diana Ross, Queen and Jane Fonda. On record, onstage, on TV and screen, Michael Jackson has no trouble stepping out. Nothing scares him, he says. But this. . . .

"Do you *like* doing this?" Michael asks. There is a note of incredulity in his voice, as though he were asking the question of a coroner. He is slumped in a dining-room chair, looking down into the lower level of the living room. It is filled with statuary. There are some graceful, Greco-Roman type bronzes, as well as a few pieces from the suburban birdbath school. The figures are frozen around the sofa like some ghostly tea party.

Michael himself is having little success sitting still. He is so nervous that he is eating – plowing through – a bag of potato chips. This is truly odd behavior. None of his brothers can recall seeing anything snacky pass his lips since he became a strict vegetarian and health-food disciple six years ago. In fact, Katherine Jackson, his mother, worries that Michael seems to exist on little more than air. As far as she can tell, her son just has no interest in food. He says that if he didn't have to eat to stay alive, he wouldn't.

"I really do hate this," he says. Having polished off the chips, he has begun to fold and refold a newspaper clipping. "I am much more relaxed onstage than I am right now. But hey, let's go." He smiles. Later, he will explain that "let's go" is what his

bodyguard always says when they are about to wade into some public fray. It's also a phrase Michael has been listening for since he was old enough to tie his own shoes.

At 24, Michael Jackson has one foot planted firmly on either side of the Eighties. His childhood hits are golden oldies, and his boyhood idols have become his peers. Michael was just 10 when he moved into Diana Ross' Hollywood home. Now he produces her. He was five when the Beatles crossed over; now he and McCartney wrangle over the same girl on Michael's single "The Girl Is Mine." His showbiz friends span generations as well. He hangs out with the likes of such other kid stars as Tatum O'Neal and Kristy McNichol, and ex-kid star Stevie Wonder. He gossips long distance with Adam Ant and Liza Minnelli, and has heart-to-hearts with octogenarian Fred Astaire. When he visited the set of *On Golden Pond*, Henry Fonda baited fishhooks for him. Jane Fonda is helping him learn acting. Pen pal Katharine Hepburn broke a lifelong habit of avoiding rock by attending a 1981 Jacksons concert at Madison Square Garden.

Even E.T. would be attracted to such a gentle spirit, according to Steven Spielberg, who says he told Michael, "If E.T. didn't come to Elliott, he would have come to your house." Spielberg also says he thought of no one else to narrate the saga of his timorous alien. "Michael is one of the last living innocents who is in complete control of his life. I've never seen *anybody* like Michael. He's an emotional star child."

Cartoons are flashing silently across the giant screen that glows in the darkened den. Michael mentions that he loves cartoons. In fact, he loves all things "magic." This definition is wide enough to include everything from Bambi to James Brown.

CIRCLE OF FRIENDS
By the early 1980s, Jackson's childhood idols had become his peers. Clockwise from top left: With Liza Minnelli in 1983 – "I consider her a great show-business friend," he said; with Paul McCartney in 1983; with Chuck Berry – whose songs he grew up listening to – at the 1978 Grammys; with actress Tatum O'Neal in 1978.

"He's *so* magic," Michael says of Brown, admitting that he patterned his own quicksilver choreography on the Godfather's classic bag of stage moves. "I'd be in the wings when I was like six or seven. I'd sit there and watch him."

Michael's kindergarten was the basement of the Apollo Theater in Harlem. He was too shy to actually approach the performers the Jackson 5 opened for – everyone from Jackie Wilson to Gladys Knight, the Temptations and Etta James. But he says he had to know everything they did – how James Brown could do a slide, a spin and a split and still make it back before the mike hit the floor. How the mike itself disappeared through the Apollo stage floor. He crept downstairs, along passageways and walls and hid there, peering from behind the dusty flanks of old vaudeville sets while musicians tuned, smoked, played cards and divvied barbecue. Climbing back to the wings, he stood in the protective folds of the musty maroon curtain, watching his favorite acts, committing every double dip and every bump, snap, whip-it-back mike toss to his inventory of

night moves. Recently, for a refresher course, Michael went to see James Brown perform at an L.A. club. "He's the *most* electrifying. He can take an audience anywhere he wants to. The audience just went bananas. He went wild – and at his age. He gets so *out* of himself."

Getting out of oneself is a recurrent theme in Michael's life, whether the subject is dancing, singing or acting. As a Jehovah's Witness, Michael believes in an impending holocaust, which will be followed by the second coming of Christ. Religion is a large part of his life, requiring intense Bible study and thrice-weekly meetings at a nearby Kingdom Hall. He has never touched drugs and rarely goes near alcohol. Still, despite the prophesied Armageddon, the spirit is not so dour as to rule out frequent hops on the fantasy shuttle.

"I'm a collector of cartoons," he says. "All the Disney stuff, Bugs Bunny, the old MGM ones. I've only met one person who has a bigger collection than I do, and I was surprised – Paul McCartney. He's a cartoon fanatic. Whenever I go to his house, we watch cartoons. When we came here to work on my album, we rented all these cartoons from the studio, *Dumbo* and some other stuff. It's real escapism. It's like everything's all right. It's like the world is happening now in a faraway city. Everything's fine.

"The first time I saw *E.T.*, I melted through the whole thing," he says. "The second time, I cried like crazy. And then, in doing the narration, I felt like I was there with them, like behind a tree or something, watching everything that happened."

So great was Michael's emotional involvement that Steven Spielberg found his narrator crying in the darkened studio when he got to the part where E.T. is dying. Finally, Spielberg and producer Quincy Jones decided to run with it and let Michael's voice break. Fighting those feelings would be counterproductive – something Jones had already learned while producing *Off the Wall*.

"I had a song I'd been saving for Michael called 'She's Out of My Life,'" he remembers. "Michael heard it, and it clicked. But when he sang it, he would cry. Every time we did it, I'd look up at the end and Michael would be crying. I said, 'We'll come back in two weeks and do it again, and maybe it won't tear you up so much.' Came back and he started to get teary. So we left it in."

This tug of war between the controlled professional and the vulnerable, private Michael surfaces in the lyrics he has written for himself. In "Bless His Soul," a song on the Jacksons' *Destiny* LP that Michael says is definitely about him, he sings:

Sometimes I cry 'cause I'm confused
Is this a fact of being used?
There is no life for me at all
'Cause I give myself at beck and call.

Two of the Jackson-written cuts on *Thriller* strengthen that defensive stance. "They eat off of you, you're a vegetable," he shouts on "Wanna Be Startin' Somethin'." "Beat It," a tense, tough dance cut, flirts with paranoia: "You have to show them that you're really not scared/You're playin' with your life, this ain't no truth or dare/They'll kick you, then they beat you/Then they'll tell you it's fair."

Yes, he says, he feels used, declining specifics, saying only that in his profession, "They demand that, and they want you to do this. They think that they own you, they think they *made* you. If you don't have faith, you go crazy. Like not doing interviews. If I talk, I say what's on my mind, and it can seem strange to other people's ears. I'm the kind of person who will tell it all, even though it's a secret. And I *know* that things should be kept private."

For his own protection, Michael has rigged himself a set of emotional floodgates, created situations where it's OK to let it all out. "Some circumstances require me to be real quiet," he says. "But I dance *every* Sunday." On that day, he also fasts.

This, his mother confirms, is a weekly ritual that leaves her son laid out, sweating, laughing and crying. It is also a ritual very similar to Michael's performances. Indeed, the weight of the Jacksons' stage show rests heavily on his narrow, sequined shoulders. There is nothing tentative about his solo turns. He can tuck his long, thin frame into a figure skater's spin without benefit of ice or skates. Aided by the burn and flash of silvery body suits, he seems to change molecular structure at will, all robot angles one second and rippling curves the next. So sure is the body that his eyes are often closed, his face turned upward to some unseen muse. The bony chest heaves. He pants, bumps and squeals. He has been known to leap offstage and climb up into the rigging.

HOLLYWOOD ROYALTY
With Brooke Shields and "Webster" star Emmanuel Lewis after the 1984 Grammys in Los Angeles

At home, in his room, he dances until he falls down. Michael says the Sunday dance sessions are also an effective way to quiet his stage addiction when he is not touring. Sometimes in these off periods, another performer will call him up from the audience. And in the long, long trip from his seat to the stage, the two Michaels duke it out.

"I sit there and say, '*Please* don't call me up, I am *too* shy,'" Jackson says. "But once I get up there, I take control of myself. Being onstage is magic. There's nothing like it. You feel the energy of everybody who's out there. You feel it all over your body. When the lights hit you, it's all over, I *swear* it is."

He is smiling now, sitting upright, trying to explain weightlessness to the earth-bound.

"When it's time to go off, I don't want to. I could stay up there forever. It's the same thing with making a movie. What's wonderful about a film is that you can become another person. I love to forget. And lots of times, you totally forget. It's like automatic pilot. I mean – whew."

During shooting for *The Wiz*, he became so attached to his Scarecrow character, the crew literally had to wrench him from the set and out of his costume. He was in Oz, and wasn't keen on leaving it for another hotel room.

"That's what I loved about doing *E.T.* I was actually there. The next day, I missed him a lot. I wanted to go back to that spot I was at yesterday in the forest. I wanted to be there."

Alas, he is still at the dining-room table in his condo. But despite the visible strain, he's holding steady. And he bright-

ens at a question about his animals. He says he talks to his menagerie every day. "I have two fawns. Mr. Tibbs looks like a ram; he's got the horns. I've got a beautiful llama. His name is Louie." He's also into exotic birds like macaws, cockatoos and a giant rhea.

"Stay right there," he says, "and I'll show you something." He takes the stairs to his bedroom two at a time. Though I know we are the only people in the apartment, I hear him talking.

"Aw, were you asleep? I'm sorry. . . ."

Seconds later, an eight-foot boa constrictor is deposited on the dining-room table. He is moving in my direction at an alarming rate.

"This is Muscles. And I have trained him to eat interviewers."

Muscles, having made it to the tape recorder and flicked his tongue disdainfully, continues on toward the nearest source of warm blood. Michael thoughtfully picks up the reptile as its snub nose butts my wrist.

Really, he insists, Muscles is quite sweet. It's all nonsense, this stuff about snakes eating people. Besides, Muscles isn't even hungry; he enjoyed his weekly live rat a couple of days ago. If anything, the stranger's presence has probably made Muscles a trifle nervous himself.

Coiled around his owner's torso, his tensile strength has made Michael's forearm a vivid bas-relief of straining blood vessels. To demonstrate the snake's sense of balance, Michael sets him down on a three-inch-wide banister, where he will remain, motionless, for the next hour or so.

"Snakes are very misunderstood," he says. Snakes, I suggest, may be the oldest victims of bad press. Michael whacks the table and laughs.

"Bad press. Ain't it *so*, Muscles?"

The snake lifts its head momentarily, then settles back on the banister. All three of us are a bit more relaxed.

"Know what I also love?" Michael volunteers. "Mannequins."

Yes, he means the kind you see wearing mink bikinis in Beverly Hills store windows. When his new house is finished, he says, he'll have a room with no furniture, just a desk and a bunch of store dummies.

"I guess I want to bring them to life. I like to imagine talking to them. You know what I think it is? Yeah, I think I'll say it. I think I'm accompanying myself with friends I never had. I probably have two friends. And I just got them. Being an entertainer, you just can't tell who is your friend. And they see you so differently. A star instead of a next-door neighbor."

He pauses, staring down at the living-room statues.

"That's what it is. I surround myself with people I want to be my friends. And I can do that with mannequins. I'll talk to them."

All of this is not to say that Michael is friendless. On the contrary, people are clamoring to be his friend. That's the trouble: with such staggering numbers knocking at the gate, it becomes necessary to sort and categorize. Michael never had a school chum. Or a playmate. Or a steady girlfriend. The two mystery friends he mentioned are his first civilians. As for the rest . . .

"I know people in show business."

Foremost is Diana Ross, with whom he shares his "deepest, darkest secrets" and problems. But even when they are alone together, their world is circumscribed. And there's Quincy Jones, "who I think is wonderful. But to get out of the realm of show business, to become like everybody else . . ."

To forget. To get out of the performing self.

"Me and Liza, say. Now, I would consider her a great friend, but a show-business friend. And we're sitting there talking about this movie, and she'll tell me all about Judy Garland. And then she'll go, 'Show me that stuff you did at rehearsal.'" He feints a dance move. "And I'll go, 'Show me yours.' We're totally into each other's *performance*."

This Michael does not find odd, or unacceptable. It's when celebrity makes every gesture a performance that he runs for cover. Some stars simply make up their minds to get on with things, no matter what. Diana Ross marched bravely into a Manhattan shoe store with her three daughters and had them fitted for running shoes, despite the crowd of 200 that convened on the sidewalk. Michael, who's been a boy in a bubble since the age of reason, would find that intolerable. He will go to only one L.A. restaurant, a health-food place where the owners know him. As for shopping, Michael avoids it by having a secretary or aide pick out clothes for him. "You don't get peace in a shop. If they don't know your name, they know your voice. And you can't hide."

He won't say love stinks. But sometimes it smarts.

"Being mobbed *hurts*. You feel like you're spaghetti among thousands of hands. They're just ripping you and pulling your hair. And you feel that any moment you're gonna just break."

Thus, Michael must travel with the veiled secrecy of a pasha's prized daughter. Any tourism is attempted from behind shades, tinted limo glass and a bodyguard's somber serge. Even in a hotel room, he hears females squeal and scurry like so many mice in the walls.

"Girls in the lobby, coming up the stairway. You hear guards getting them out of elevators. But you stay in your room and write a song. And when you get tired of that, you talk to yourself. Then let it all out onstage. *That's* what it's like."

No argument – it ain't natural. But about those store dummies? Won't it be just as eerie to wake up in the middle of the night to all those polystyrene grins?

"Oh, I'll give them names. Like the statues you see down there." He motions to the living-room crowd. "They've got names. I feel as if I know them. I'll go down there and talk to them."

A restless rhythm is jiggling his foot, and the newspaper clipping has long been destroyed. Michael is apologetic, explaining that he can sit still for just so long. On an impulse, he decides to drive us to the house under construction. Though his parents forced him to learn two years ago, Michael rarely drives. When he does, he refuses to travel freeways, taking hour-long detours to avoid them. He has learned the way to only a few "safe" zones – his brothers' homes, the health-food restaurant and the Kingdom Hall.

First, Muscles must be put away. "He's real sweet," Michael says as he unwinds the serpent from the banister. "I'd like you to wrap him around you before you go."

This is not meant as a prank, and Michael will not force the issue. But fear of interviews can be just as deep-rooted as fear of snakes, and in consenting to talk, Michael was told the same thing he's telling me now: *Trust me. It won't hurt you.*

We compromise. Muscles cakewalks across an ankle. His tongue is dry. It just tickles. Block out the primal dread, and it could be a kitten whisker. "You truly believe," says Michael, "with the power of reason, that this animal won't harm you now, right? But there's this fear, built in by the world, by what people say, that makes you shy away like that."

Having politely made their point, Michael and Muscles disappear upstairs.

'H I, MICHAEL."
A few such girlish messages are scratched into the paint of a somber security sign on the steel driveway gate at his house. There is a fence, dogs and guards, but girls still will loiter outside, in cars and in bushes.

As Michael conducts the tour of the two-story Tudor-style house, it's clear that the room he will sleep in is almost monkish compared to those he has had designed for his pleasures and the ones reserved for his sisters Janet and La Toya, who pored over every detail of their wallpapered suites. "Girls are fussy," he explains, stepping over a power saw in his bedroom. "I just don't care. I wanted room to dance and have my books."

The rooms Michael inspects most carefully are those marked for recreation. "I'm putting all this stuff in," he says, "so I will never have to leave and go out *there*." The "stuff" includes a screening room with two professional projectors and a giant speaker. And then an exercise room, one for video games and another with a giant-screen video system. In addition, there is a huge chamber off the backyard patio, which has been designated the Pirate Room. It will be not so much decorated as populated. More dummies. But this set will talk back. Michael has been consulting with a Disney technician, the very man who designed the Audio-Animatronics figures for the Disneyland ride Pirates of the Caribbean. If all goes well, he will install several scowling, scabbard-waving buccaneers, wenches and sea dogs right here. "There won't be any rides," Michael says. "But there will be a pirate shootout, cannons and guns. They'll just scream at one another, and I'll have the lights, sounds, everything."

Pirates is one of his favorite rides in the Magic Kingdom. And Disneyland is one of the few public spots even he cannot stay away from. Sometimes Michael stops at a magic booth and buys one of those Groucho masks – fake glasses with nose attached. But it's better when the staff leads him through back doors and tunnels. It's murder to cross the court of Sleeping Beauty's Castle in daylight. "I tried to go just last night, but it was closed," he says with some disbelief. "So was Knott's Berry Farm."

If you live in the funhouse, you usually don't have to worry about such things. Michael has sung it himself:

Life ain't so bad at all, if you live it off the wall.

When we arrive back at the condo, Michael finds that a test pressing of "The Girl Is Mine" has been delivered. This is business. He must check it before release, he explains, as he heads for a listen on the stereo in the den. Before the record is finished, he is punching at phone buttons. In between calls to accountants and managers, he says that he makes all his own decisions, right down to the last sequin on his stage suits – the only clothes he cares about. He says he can be a merciless interviewer when it comes to choosing management, musicians and concert promoters. He assesses their performances with the rigor of an investigative reporter, questioning his brothers, fellow artists and even reporters for observations. Though he truly believes his talent comes from God, he is acutely aware of its value on the open market. He is never pushy or overbearing, but he does appreciate respect. Do not ask him, for instance, how long he has been with a particular show-business firm. "Ask me," he corrects, "how long they've been with *me*."

Those who have worked with him do not doubt his capability. Even those to whom he is a star child. "He's in full control," says Spielberg. "Sometimes he appears to other people to be sort of wavering on the fringes of twilight, but there is great conscious forethought behind everything he does. He's very smart about his career and the choices he makes. I think he is definitely a man of two personalities."

When Michael was looking for a producer for his solo album, Quincy Jones was happy to hear from him. Jones knew Michael was in a special class. A few things tipped him off, he says. First there was the Academy Awards ceremony at which Jones watched 14-year-old Michael deliver a trash-flick love song to a fascist rodent ("Ben") with astounding poise. Years later, while working with him on the *Wiz* soundtrack, Jones says, "I saw another side. Watching him in the context of being an actor, I saw a lot of things about him as a singer that rang a lot of bells. I saw a depth that was never apparent, and a commitment. I saw that Michael was growing up."

In the studio, Jones found that his professionalism had matured. In fact, Michael's nose for things is so by-your-leave funky that Jones started calling him Smelly. Fortunately, when corporate rumblings feared the partnership too unlikely to work, Smelly hung tough and cocked an ear inward to his own special rhythms. Indeed, *Off the Wall*'s most memorable cuts are the Jackson-penned dance tunes. "Working Day and Night," with all its breathy asides and deft punctuation, could only have been written by a dancer. "Don't Stop 'Til You Get Enough," the album's biggest-selling single, bops along with that same appealing give-and-go between restraint and abandon. The song begins with Michael talking in a low mumble over a taut, single-string bass bomp:

You know, I was wonderin'. . . . You know the force, it's got a lot of power, make me feel like a . . . make me feel like. . . ."

Ooooooh. Fraidy cat breaks into disco monster, with onrushing strings and a sexy, cathartic squeal. The introduction is 10 seconds of perfect pop tension. Dance boogie is the welcome release. The arrangement – high, gusting strings and vocals over a thudding, in-the-pocket rhythm – is Michael's signature. Smelly, the funky sprite.

It works. Such a creature as Michael is the perfect pop hybrid for the Eighties. The fanzine set is not scared off by raunchy lyrics and chest hair. But the R-rated uptown dance crowd can bump and slide right along the greasy tracks. *Thriller* is eclectic enough to include African chants and some ripping macho-rock guitar work by Eddie Van Halen. It is now being called pop-soul by those into marketing categories. Michael says he doesn't care what anybody wants to call it. Just how it all came about is still a mystery to him – as is the creative process itself.

"I wake up from dreams and go, 'Wow, put *this* down on paper,'" he says. "The whole thing is strange. You hear the words, everything is right there in front of your face. And you say to yourself, 'I'm sorry, I just didn't write this. It's there already.' That's why I hate to take credit for the songs I've written. I feel that somewhere, someplace, it's been done and I'm just a courier bringing it into the world. I really believe that. I love what I do. I'm happy at what I do. It's escapism."

Again, that word. But Michael is right. There is no better definition for good, well-meaning, American pop. Few understand this better than Diana Ross, that Tamla teen turned latter-day pop diva. Her closeness to Michael began when she met the Jacksons.

"No, I didn't discover them," she says, countering the myth. Motown head Berry Gordy had already found them; she simply introduced them on her 1971 television special. "There was an identification between Michael and I," she says. "I was older, he kind of idolized me, and he wanted to sing like me."

She has been pleased to watch Michael become his own person. Still, she wishes he would step out even more. She says she had to be firm and force him to stay in his role as producer on "Muscles." He wanted them to do it jointly. She insisted he go it alone.

"He spends a lot of time, too much time, by himself. I try to get him out. I rented a boat and took my children and Michael on a cruise. Michael has a lot of people around him, but he's very afraid. I don't know why. I think it came from the early days."

Michael's show-business friends, many of them women not thought of as especially motherly, do go to great lengths to push and prod him into the world, and to keep him comfortable. When he's in Manhattan, Ross urges him to go to the theater and the clubs, and counteroffers with quiet weekends at her Connecticut home. In notes and phone calls, Katharine Hepburn has been encouraging about his acting.

Michael has recorded much of this counsel in notebooks and on tape. Visiting Jane Fonda – whom he's known since they met at a Hollywood party a few years ago – on the New Hampshire set of *On Golden Pond* proved to be an intensive crash course. In a mirror version of his scenes with the stepgrandson in the movie, Henry Fonda took his daughter's rock-star friend out on the lake and showed him how to fish. They sat on a jetty for hours, talking trout and theater. The night Fonda died, Michael spent the evening with Fonda's widow, Shirlee, and his children,

Jane and Peter. He says they sat around, laughing and crying and watching the news reports. The ease with which Michael was welcomed into her family did not surprise Jane Fonda. Michael and her father got on naturally, she says, because they were so much alike.

"Dad was also painfully self-conscious and shy in life," she says, "and he really only felt comfortable when he was behind the mask of a character. He could liberate himself when he was being someone else. That's a lot like Michael.

"In some ways," she continues, "Michael reminds me of the walking wounded. He's an extremely fragile person. I think that just getting on with life, making contact with people, is hard enough, much less to be worried about whither goest the world.

"I remember driving with him one day, and I said, 'God, Michael, I wish I could find a movie I could produce for you.' And suddenly I knew. I said, 'I know what you've got to do. It's *Peter Pan.*' Tears welled up in his eyes and he said, 'Why did you say that?' with this *ferocity.* I said, 'I realize *you're* Peter Pan.' And he started to cry and said, 'You know, all over the walls of my room are pictures of Peter Pan. I've read everything that [author J.M.] Barrie wrote. I totally identify with Peter Pan, the lost boy of never-never land.'"

Hearing that Francis Coppola may be doing a film version, Fonda sent word to him that he must talk to Michael Jackson. "Oh, I can see him," she says, "leading lost children into a world of fantasy and magic."

In the book, that fantasy world lies "second to the right star, then straight on 'til morning" – no less strange a route, Fonda notes, than Michael's own journey from Indiana.

"From Gary," she says, "straight on to Barrie."

IN THE SPOTLIGHT
Jackson performs in 1981. "Being onstage is magic," he told Rolling Stone. "When it's time to go off, I don't want to. I could stay up there forever."

'ALL CHILDREN, EXCEPT ONE, GROW UP."
This is the first line of Michael's favorite book, and if you ask Katherine Jackson if she finds this similar to what happened in her own brood of nine, she will laugh and say, oh yes, her fifth son is the one.

Five children – Maureen, Tito, Jackie, Jermaine and Marlon – are married and have families. La Toya is a very independent young woman. At 13, Janet was starring as a self-possessed ghetto twerp on the sitcom *Good Times.* Now she has a hit single of her own, "Young Love," and appears in the sitcom *Diff'rent Strokes.* Youngest brother Randy is already living on his own at 20. Michael is sure he'd just die if he tried that.

"La Toya once told me she thinks that I overprotected them all," Mrs. Jackson says. "But under the circumstances, I truly don't think so."

After her marriage, she set up her household in the chilly industrial town of Gary, Indiana, just outside of Chicago. A growing family had forced Joe Jackson to disband the Falcons, an R&B group he had formed with his two brothers. Playing Chuck

Berry and Fats Domino covers in local clubs was as far as they got. The guitar went into the closet, and Jackson went to the steel mills as a crane operator. The family budget didn't have a lot of slack for toys, but there was an old saxophone, a tambourine, some bongos and a homey patchwork of songs from Katherine's childhood. What she could remember, she taught her children. "It was just plain stuff," she says, "like 'Cotton Fields' and 'You Are My Sunshine.'"

The breadth of the harmony grew with the family. Jackie, Jermaine and Tito started singing together, with Tito on guitar and Jermaine on bass. Then Marlon climbed aboard. Baby Michael, who liked to flail on the bongos, surprised his mother one day when she heard him imitating Jermaine's lead vocals in his clear toddler's falsetto. "I think we have another lead singer," she told her husband. The brothers agreed.

"He was so energetic that at five years old, he was like a leader," says Jackie, at 31 the oldest brother. "We saw that. So we said, 'Hey, Michael, you be the lead guy.' The audience ate it up. He was into those James Brown things at the time, you know. The speed was the thing. He would see somebody do something, and he could do it right away."

"It was sort of frightening," his mother says. "He was so young. He didn't go out and play much. So if you want me to tell you the truth, I don't know where he got it. He just *knew*."

By the age of seven, Michael was a dance monster, working out the choreography for the whole group. Local gigs were giving way to opening slots at larger halls in distant cities. Joe Jackson spent weekends and evenings as chauffeur, road manager, agent and coach. He taught Michael how to work a stage and handle a mike. Michael does not remember his father making it fun; the boys always knew it was work. Rules were strict. Grades had to be kept up, even with five shows a night, or the offender would be yanked off the road. When Motown called, Joe took the boys to Detroit, and Katherine stayed in Gary with the rest of the children. She says she never really worried about her children until she went to a show and heard the screams from the audience. "Every time I'd go to a concert I'd worry, because sometimes the girls would get onstage and I'd have to watch them tearing at Michael," Katherine says. "He was so small, and they were so big."

There have been some serious incidents, too, one so chilling and bizarre it landed a young woman in a mental institution. So Katherine Jackson has made it her business to talk to some of these wild, persistent girls. What is so very crazy, she says, is that they do it in the name of love. "There are so many," she says. "You have no idea what's really on their minds. That's why it's going to be so hard for my son to get a wife."

Michael is aware of, if not resigned to, the impossibility of that task. He might like to have children in the future, but says he would probably adopt them. For now, he has only to walk into one of his brothers' homes and he's instantly covered with nephews. He says he gets along with children better than adults, anyhow: "They don't wear masks."

Kids and animals can nose their way into Michael's most private reserves. It's the showbiz spook show that makes his own

growing up so public and hard. He has borne, with patience and good humor, the standard rumors of sex-change operations and paternity accusations from women he has never seen. But clearly they have affected him. "Billie Jean," on *Thriller*, is a vehement denial of paternity ("the kid is not my son"). In reality there has been no special one. Michael says that he is not in a hurry to jump into any romantic liaison.

"It's like what I told you about finding friends," he says. "With *that*, it's even harder. With so many girls around, how am I ever gonna *know*?"

'J UST HERE TO SEE A FRIEND." Michael is politely trying to sidestep an inquiring young woman decked out with the latest video equipment. She blocks the corridor leading to the warren of dressing rooms beneath the L.A. Forum. "Can I tell my viewers that Michael Jackson is a Queen fan?"

"I'm a Freddie Mercury fan," he says, slipping past her into a long room crowded with Queen band members, wives, roadies and friends. A burly man with the look of a linebacker is putting lead singer Freddie Mercury through a set of stretching exercises that will propel his road-weary muscles through the final show of the group's recent U.S. tour. The band is merry. Michael is shy, standing quietly at the door until Freddie spots him and leaps up to gather him in a hug.

Freddie invited Michael. He has been calling all week, mainly about the possibility of their working together. They've decided to try it on the Jacksons' upcoming album. Though they are hardly alike – Freddie celebrated a recent birthday by hanging naked from a chandelier – the two have been friendly since Michael listened to the material Queen had recorded for *The Game* and insisted that the single had to be "Another One Bites the Dust."

"Now, he listens to me, right, Freddie?"

"Righto, little brother."

The linebacker beckons. Freddie waves his cigarette at the platters of fruit, fowl and candy. "You and your friends make yourselves comfortable."

Our escort, a sweet-faced, hamfisted bodyguard, is consulting with security about seat locations. There had been girls lurking outside the condo when Michael sprinted to the limousine, girls peering through the tinted glass as the door locks clicked shut. This was all very puzzling to Michael's guest, who was waiting in the car.

He is a real friend, one of the civilians, so normal as to pass unseen by the jaded eyes of celebrity watchers. He has never been to a rock concert, nor has he ever seen Michael perform. He says he hopes to, but mainly, they just hang out together. Sometimes his younger brother even tags along. Most of the time they just talk "just regular old stuff," says the friend. For Michael, it is another kind of magic.

At the moment, though, it's show business as usual. Gossip, to be specific. Michael is questioning a dancer he knows about the recent crises of a fallen superstar. Michael wants to know

PRIZE POSSESSIONS
*Michael and Quincy Jones at the Grammys on
February 28th, 1984, the night he won a record-setting
eight awards, including Album of the Year for "Thriller."*

what the problem is. The dancer mimes his answer, laying a finger alongside his nose. Michael nods, and translates for his friend: "Drugs. Cocaine."

Michael admits that he seeks out such gossip, and listens again and again as the famous blurt out their need for escape. "Escapism," he says. "I totally understand."

But addictions are another thing. "I always want to know what makes good performers fall to pieces," he says. "I always try to find out. Because I just can't believe it's the same things that get them time and time again." So far, his own addictions – the stage, dancing, cartoons – have been free of toxins.

Something's working on Michael now, but it is nothing chemical. He's buzzing like a bumblebee trapped in a jelly jar. It's the room we're in, he explains. So many times, he's stretched and bounced and whipped up on his vocal cords right here, got crazy in here, pumping up, shivering like some flighty race horse as he wriggled into his sequined suit.

"I can't *stand* this," he fairly yells. "I cannot sit still."

Just before he must be held down for his own good, Randy Jackson rockets into the room, containing his brother in a bear hug, helping him dissipate some of the energy with a short bout of wrestling. This is not the same creature who tried to hide behind a potato chip.

Now Michael is boxing with the bodyguard, asking every minute for the time until the man mercifully claps a big hand on the shoulder of his charge and says it: "Let's go."

Mercury and company have already begun moving down the narrow hall, and before anyone can catch him, Michael is drawn into their wake, riding on the low roar of the crowd outside, leaping up to catch a glimpse of Freddie, who is raising a fist and about to take the stairs to the stage.

"Ooooh, Freddie is pumped," says Michael. "I envy him now. You don't *know* how much."

The last of the band makes the stairs, and the black stage curtain closes. Michael turns and lets himself be led into the darkness of the arena.

131

BIGGER, TOUGHER, RISKIER

Michael took two years to make his next album,
with one goal: Beat 'Thriller.' By Jon Dolan

TOUGHER THAN LEATHER
*Michael during the "Bad" tour,
which drew 4.5 million fans from
September 1987 to January 1989*

MICHAEL JACKSON WAS NEVER SHY ABOUT THE ONE GREAT GOAL OF HIS post-*Thriller* career: outsell *Thriller.* Producer Quincy Jones, who returned to handle *Bad,* wasn't so sure. "Figuring out how to sell 38 million albums?" he said in 1987. "I don't know how to do that. That's in God's hands." ★ If *Bad* hadn't been overshadowed by its expectations, its hype, its budget – if it had just been received as 11 songs by a great artist – it might have been considered a masterpiece. It's Jackson's last truly great record, one that brilliantly balances his pop-soul pinup side with his angry, alienated side. ★ "Michael wanted to make a tough record," recalled Jones. It was a good time for an overhaul. The Jacksons' 1984 *Victory* tour, despite grossing $75 million, had been a career low point. Tickets were so expensive that

Jackson publicly apologized in a pre-tour press conference, and the show itself was marred by embarrassing staging and silly special effects (such as Michael being chased around by a giant spider). Jackson's tabloid travails were beginning to loom bigger than his music: the pet llama, his bosom buddy Bubbles the chimp, the hyperbaric chamber, the quest to buy the Elephant Man's bones. Jackson's own manager, Frank DiLeo, admitted Michael had become "a cross between E.T. and Howard Hughes."

The Jackson on *Bad* was harder, less cuddly, ratcheting up the music's intensity. The beats had wicked pistol pop, the rock guitars were torrid, and the synth textures were shadowy and sleek. It was like *Thriller* on steroids: The Stevie Wonder duet "Just Good Friends" reworked the formula from Jackson's duet with Paul McCartney "The Girl Is Mine." "Liberian Girl" snagged a groove from "Billie Jean." "Leave Me Alone" was the first of Jackson's anti-media screeds (in the video, he sings from inside the pages of tabloid papers); "Smooth Criminal" had gangster imagery and intimations of violence, playing with Jackson's rep as a "safe" black artist. Even the happy refrain on the poppy soul number "The Way You Make Me Feel" – "It ain't nobody's business" – had a newfound hardness.

This also translated to more rock & roll. "He kept asking me about rock bands: 'Do you know Mötley Crüe?'" recalls guitarist Steve Stevens, who played on the album's metal-tinged "Dirty Diana." "A couple weeks later I saw Eddie Van Halen, and I told him I'd been working with Michael. Eddie said, 'Did he like the high notes?' And Michael did – he liked that rock & roll screech. When we met, I was wearing patent leather, he was wearing penny loafers. I turned him on to the guy who did my clothes."

Compared with *Thriller,* which took three months, *Bad* took more than two years to make and cost $2 million. Jackson had 62 songs written and wanted to release 33 of them as a triple album, until Jones talked him down. The carnivalesque world Jackson inhabited crept into the sessions at Los Angeles' Westlake Audio Studios. Bubbles rode around on the engineer's Great Dane, and Crusher, Jackson's 300-pound, 20-foot python, gave keyboardist Greg Phillinganes a "small heart attack," according to Jones.

Pals like Oprah Winfrey and Robert De Niro came by to offer moral support, while Jackson and Jones laid down take after take, seeking perfection. "There was so much stress," said guitarist David Williams. "I was doing the exact same part at least five different times on each song."

Attempts to wrangle superstar collaborations were just as problematic. Jones had conceived "Bad" (which had the working title "Pee") as a duet with Prince, imagining a blockbuster video in which the Purple One and MJ square off "like fighters." Jones arranged a summit between the two, but Prince demurred after hearing the song. "It will be a big hit even if I'm not on it," he told Jackson as he left their meeting. Barbra Streisand turned down the ballad duet "I Just Can't Stop Loving You."

One of the album's final additions was "Man in the Mirror." Songwriter Glen Ballard had buttonholed Jones at a party and asked if he still needed new Michael songs. "Yeah," Jones exclaimed. "I need a hit!"

"They were closing out the record, and Quincy said, 'Don't you have anything for us?'" Ballard says. "So Siedah Garrett wrote 'Man in the Mirror' on a Saturday night at my house in Encino. We didn't have a chance to dress it up, so I didn't feel like it had a chance, but Quincy played it for Michael, and he said, 'Make a track.' The song was this really magical moment, and it had everything to do with Michael's vocal interpretation. In the last two minutes, Michael started doing these incantations: all the *'shamons'* and *'oohs.'* He went to that place on his own. We certainly couldn't have written that."

Garrett got an extra surprise when she ended up singing with Jackson on "I Just Can't Stop Loving You." She thought she was coming into the studio to listen to a final mix of "Man in the Mirror," and was sitting there knitting when Jones asked her to step into the vocal booth. There she saw music stands with music labeled with her name and Jackson's name, and Jackson walked into the booth beside her.

To loosen things up and find his groove, Jackson danced around the vocal booth before singing his lyrics. "I'd be looking through a window [into the vocal booth], which was totally

HIT SQUAD
*Jackson, Jones and
engineer Bruce Swedien
(from left) at Westlake
Studios, 1986*

dark," engineer Bruce Swedien says, describing the session for "The Way You Make Me Feel." "I could only see the mike. He'd sing his line, then he'd disappear into the darkness. But when it was time to sing a line he'd be right back in front of the mike at the precise moment."

"That was one of my favorites," recalls Phillinganes of "The Way You Make Me Feel." "It's a really intense shuffle. I remember how much fun I had laying down those offbeat parts, the bass line, all that stuff, and watching the expression on Michael's face – he'd get that big grin that meant you had it."

When the album was finally finished, CBS Records pulled out all the stops promoting it. The title track was licensed to Pepsi to be used in one commercial, a four-minute performance clip that advised soft-drink consumers: "I'm bad, I'm bad, I'm bad…and Pepsi's cool!" CBS Records promoted the album with a half-hour special on its sister TV network, pre-emptively titled *Michael Jackson…The Magic Returns.* CBS flew 50 radio and retail high rollers to Los Angeles, where they listened to the album at the Beverly Hills Hotel's Crystal Ballroom before being whisked to a dinner at Jackson's brand-new home, Neverland.

Bad's cover made sure consumers got the message about Jackson's manly new identity: An airbrushed photo of Michael's made-up face framed by black floral lace was replaced at the last minute with a downright butch shot of him as a leather hunk against a stark white backdrop. The new Michael got

ROMAN HOLIDAY
Michael in Rome with the local police, May 1988. Jackson reportedly spent one night in Rome walking the streets in a wig and mustache.

his all-important MTV debut in the video for "Bad," which went for street cred. Jackson hoped to get George Lucas or Steven Spielberg to direct the clip, but DiLeo convinced him to go with Martin Scorsese. Filmed in Harlem and on a Brooklyn subway platform, and co-starring a young Wesley Snipes, "Bad" portrays Jackson as a prep-school kid struggling with his gang roots. The choreographer who did the fight scenes in *Raging Bull* was brought in. Jackson insisted on countless retakes – the scene where he stares down Snipes in a grungy stairwell was shot 40 times.

"We went over schedule; it was two and a half weeks of the dance sequence alone," Scorsese recalls of the gangland dance-off that comprises the meat of the video. The full unedited version clocked in at 18 minutes and stood for two decades as the longest video ever.

"He was not in it to go halfway – he really wanted to do something forever," says Ballard. "He was always thinking about that legacy." Within a year of release, *Bad* sold 6 million copies, staying on the top of the *Billboard* charts for six weeks and spawning five Number One singles.

Before Jackson started calling himself the King of Pop, he described himself with a less triumphal sobriquet, "the loneliest man in the world." The genius of *Bad* was its ability to honestly depict that alienation while creating dramatic, provocative music. The album sold 30 million copies worldwide, and if *Thriller's* 38.5 million remained out of reach, Michael proved one thing: He could fail bigger than anyone on the planet.

ON THE EDGE

Heading into the Nineties, Jackson re-emerged with a new producer and a fresh sound to make his boldest move yet. By Jon Dolan

SUPER JAM
*Michael onstage at the
Super Bowl, backed by
guitarist Jennifer
Batten, in 1993*

IN 1989, THE MUSIC INDUSTRY GATHERED AT THE "SOUL TRAIN" MUSIC AWARDS TO give something back to the man who'd helped save it in the MTV Decade. Standing onstage in front of a room full of tuxedoed eminences, Elizabeth Taylor, there to present her close friend Michael Jackson with a Heritage Award, crowned him "the true King of Pop, Rock and Soul." ★ But as Jackson accepted the award, the music world was changing around him: If the Eighties had been about one-name royals (Michael, Bruce, Madonna, Prince), the dawning Nineties would be about fragmented styles (hip-hop, grunge, industrial, techno). Michael Jackson was the biggest star with the most to lose, and his response, 1991's *Dangerous*, was his boldest move yet. Acknowledging the massive shift black music had experienced in the hip-hop

era, Jackson jettisoned Quincy Jones, the man he'd been making records with since the age of disco. "Michael was growing," remembers Bill Bottrell, a longtime collaborator of Jackson's who worked on *Dangerous*. "He didn't need to have a father-figure relationship anymore, like the one he had with Quincy. He needed to renew his sense of control and at the same time look for new things."

Jackson had been trying to find an edgier sound for a while (versions of "Black or White" had been floating around since the *Bad* days), but nothing he or his staff came up with felt right. Jones claimed he'd encouraged Jackson to consider incorporating hip-hop on 1987's *Bad*, but the singer didn't think rap had staying power. "I think he probably felt I wasn't in touch with the market," Jones recalled in a recent interview.

A search to find the hot new producer began. Jackson flew ascendant R&B songwriting team LA Reid and Kenneth "Babyface" Edmonds to Los Angeles for a meeting at Neverland. "He gave us a tour of the place," Reid recalls. "We went through every room in the house and talked about the art, the sculptures. And he was asking really interesting questions: 'What is your favorite music? Which artists do you love? What songs do you love? And what do you want to do with your career?'" Yet after three weeks of constant writing, nothing seemed to click.

The next call went out to new jack swing producer Teddy Riley, fresh off his success with Bobby Brown and Guy. Riley took charge immediately. "I came in with 10 grooves," he said at the time. "He liked them all."

Jackson was taking risks with his career as well as his music. Quincy Jones wasn't the only member of Jackson's inner circle to exit post-*Bad*. Jackson replaced flamboyant manager Frank DiLeo and split with his longtime lawyer, John Branca. His sense of isolation was deepening; his painkiller addiction would force him to curtail the subsequent *Dangerous* tour. All this and the ever-present pressure to attain his impossible sales goal ("Gotta outdo *Bad*, gotta outdo *Thriller*," he repeated constantly to associates) cranked up the tension.

Dangerous was made over two years in seven different studios. Jackson shuttled between 18-hour days working on the record and epic video shoots, leaving entire soundstages full of actors and video crews with nothing to do. The musicians and engineers didn't have such downtime. "He'd take off on us, but there was always work to do," remembers engineer Bruce Swedien, who had been working with Jackson since *Off the Wall*. "There was no deadline; we could work on mixes for weeks on end. He just had one qualification: It had to be the best possible. For *Dangerous*, I have a tape that says MIX EDIT FIVE, TEST EDIT 2. I still have hundreds of tapes like that."

Visitors weren't allowed into the studio – with certain exceptions. "One day, I came to the studio, and it was crawling with security," Swedien recalls. "Ronald and Nancy Reagan were there. They were building the Reagan Library nearby, and Michael said, 'Come over.' And when Michael says, 'Come over,' you come over. Ron was extremely quiet, and Nancy did all the talking. She adored Michael. One day, I went in and Jane Fonda was sitting in the corner. I had to play it cool as could be."

With no defined schedule and everyone on the clock, costs skyrocketed. The final total was roughly $10 million, at a time when most massive blockbusters cost a fifth of that amount. One industry insider of the era called it "beyond comprehension."

"He would sing the songs from top to bottom 20, 25 times trying to get the best take," says Reid, referring to songs that never even made the album. Guns n' Roses guitarist Slash was summoned to solo over "Give In to Me" and hummed ideas for the part over the phone.

"We met at the Record Plant in Hollywood," Slash recalls. "He was there with Brooke Shields, and I'm just this grungy little kid from Hollywood, this rock guitarist. So this was very sort of out of my league. But, you know, he was very sweet, very polite, said 'Hi,' said he and Brooke were going to have dinner, or something like that, and so we shook hands, and then he took off and left me to my business, and that was it."

Jackson's endemic niceness, while endearing him to his co-workers, could lead to impasses. An avid reader of self-help

LAY IT DOWN
Michael spent two years in seven different studios making "Dangerous."

books, he was reluctant to give negative feedback and allowed songwriters all the time they needed to flesh out ideas. Any harsh criticism was directed inward. During the recording of "Keep the Faith," a "Man in the Mirror"-style anthem of uplift, Jackson retreated to his office because he couldn't sing the song in the right key. Swedien found him standing in a corner, crying. "He was absolutely heartbroken," recalls Swedien. "He was very hard on himself."

Riley's most up-to-the-minute contribution was "Remember the Time," a wistfully nostalgic love song that contrasts new jack beats with recollections of a simpler past ("We'd stay on the phone/At night till dawn"), and alluded to a privacy and freedom Michael could no longer enjoy. "Can't Let Her Get Away" set lyrics that implied desperate, even panicked desire against a feverish, quaking groove and bristling synth stabs.

Quincy Jones' tracks were often colorful and richly orchestrated, reflecting his Hollywood background. The 24-year-old Riley went for something simpler. "We didn't just add music or instruments just to be adding," Riley remembered.

This was crystal clear on the title track. It had been in the can for a while, but the beat didn't feel right. "The music didn't move Michael," Riley said. "I told Michael, 'This is your album, Michael. If this is the right tune, let me change the whole bottom and put a new floor in there.' He said, 'Try it. I guess we gotta use what we love.'" The resulting tune was a classic-Michael attack on a skeezin' girl, mixing bright strings (a Jackson favorite) with one of the heaviest, starkest beats he'd ever sung over.

SCREAM
Michael kicked off the last leg of the "Dangerous" tour in Bangkok, August 1993.

Throughout the record, Riley forced Jackson to navigate a tense, jittery rhythmic push-and-pull. The beats are almost as high in the mix as Jackson's increasingly pinched, anguished vocals, suggesting a poignant sense of helplessness. "One day I was in the studio working, and Michael and Teddy came in and put on this track 'In the Closet,' and it was just incredible," recalls keyboardist-arranger Brad Buxer. "The song was almost atonal. I was like, 'This is the cutting-edge stuff.'"

Bottrell also worked to move Michael out of his safety zone, notably on the anti-racist rocker "Black or White," which became the album's first single. "I felt his rock stuff up to that point had been kind of cartoonish," Bottrell recalls. "He walked into the studio one day, and he hummed me this part. I don't think he intended it to be a guitar part, but it became the guitar part in the song. I turned it into a Southern-rock song, a real gutbucket-rock tune. The vocals in the song are the scratch vocals, but Michael was rocking so hard, I didn't want to change it."

Dangerous might be remembered by pop historians as the record that Nirvana's *Nevermind* famously knocked off the top of the *Billboard* charts, ringing in the alt-rock era. But the King of Pop's dread, depression and wounded-child sense of good and evil had more in common with Kurt Cobain than anyone took the time to notice.

THE THRILL IS GONE

This ambitious double album ended up being little more than a monument to Michael himself. By Jon Dolan

JACKSON WAS GOING THROUGH ONE OF THE DARKEST TIMES OF HIS LIFE IN THE early Nineties. His 1993 child-molestation lawsuit at one point involved him having his genitalia inspected and photographed by L.A. police (the suit was eventually settled out of court, reportedly for around $20 million, in early 1994). His drug problems were deepening, and his marriage to Lisa Marie Presley in May 1994, which lasted 20 months, was mocked as a publicity stunt. Angry and humiliated, Jackson decided to add an extra disc of new songs to *HIStory*, which was originally planned as a greatest-hits set. The new work evolved into a concept album about the ravages of fame and his ongoing legal travails. ★ Work on *HIStory* began in late 1993. The sessions quickly became overblown affairs, even by Jackson's standards: More than 150 people are credited on the album,

including 30 different people working on keyboards and synths. "When he first asked me to come out to the studio, it was intimidating," recalls producer Dallas Austin, who co-wrote two songs on *HIStory*. "He set me up in a studio, and there were other producers in each room, maybe R. Kelly in one, Teddy Riley in one."

Jackson also brought in more marquee-name guests than ever before, including two full-framed rappers of varying skill levels – the Notorious B.I.G., who laid down a freestyle on "This Time Around," and Shaquille O'Neal, who rapped on "2 Bad." Jackson hit up Boyz II Men for background vocals on "HIStory." He covered the Beatles' "Come Together" and Charlie Chaplin's "Smile."

What emerged was the weirdest record of Jackson's career. Previous Jackson songs had alluded to the controversy in his life, but *HIStory* went at his monstrous media image head-on. "Scream," a duet with his sister Janet, is pure fame-hate; the two seem to stand outside their lives in pure horror. On "Stranger in Moscow," he wanders past Stalin's tomb, contemplating his

"swift and sudden fall from grace," and equating himself with one of history's cruelest despots. "Tabloid Junkie" lashes out at his persecutors in the media: "With your pen you torture men/You'd crucify the Lord."

"Michael was less interested in fun than he had been on *Thriller*," recalls Bruce Swedien, who engineered the record. "He didn't want people to look at him. He was worried about the plastic surgery; people would stare."

At times, Jackson's requests bordered on the impossible: "He told me, 'I want you to manufacture sounds the human ear has never heard,'" says sound designer Chuck Wild. "I paid some guys to go down to the train tracks and spend a month recording passing trains." Wild still isn't sure where some of the hundreds of sounds he recorded ended up. "I got a credit on *Blood on the Dance Floor*, and I have no idea what it's for."

The obsessive quest to pile on sounds led to denser music, especially in terms of percussion. Songs like "Tabloid Junkie" and "They Don't Care About Us" have vicious, complex mechanically churning beats. The mean sounds fit the confrontational

OUT OF THE SPOTLIGHT
Jackson backstage in Bremen, Germany, in 1997

MAN OF STEEL
*Nine giant statues of Jackson – like this
32-foot one, on London's River Thames
– were erected across Europe.*

songs. "They Don't Care About Us" would become one of the most controversial songs of his career; Jackson sings, "Jew me, sue me/Everybody do me/Kick me, kike me/Don't you black or white me," adopting the mind-set of a bigot, a perspective shift that's almost totally lost on the listener.

"Before we started working on *HIStory*, he took everyone to the Museum of Tolerance in L.A.," says Austin. "Where he sang 'Kick me, kike me,' he was doing like they do at the museum where you try to imagine how people of different backgrounds feel, but it got turned around." On later copies of the CD those lyrics were digitally scrubbed from the music.

Other moments on *HIStory* attempt to give us a more open-hearted (and heavy-handed) version of Jackson's hurt soul. On "Earth Song," Jackson literally screams at God, backed by a choir led by Grammy-winning gospel artist Andraé Crouch. During one of the sessions, the singers surrounded Jackson and bowed in prayer. "My singers and I gathered around him and prayed that everything would settle and all the sparks would stop," Crouch said.

The emotional heart of the record was "Smile," a standard composed by one of his heroes, Charlie Chaplin. "When Michael was done, he got up on the conductor's stand and said, 'I just want to thank you for this performance,'" recalls Swedien. "They got up in unison and applauded. They tapped their bows on their music stands. Michael left the session in tears."

Jackson personally unveiled *HIStory* for the Sony brass in early 1995. The executives sat through the album and left the listening session in silence, sending Jackson's manager Sandy Gallin into a rage – "Are you all brain-dead?" he screamed as the executives filed out of the room. Jackson later turned to Swedien and tearfully said, "I'll never do this again!"

Despite any doubts about the album, *HIStory* was launched with a $30 million marketing campaign, including a $4 million promotional spot filmed in Budapest in which Jackson, in full military regalia, surveys hundreds of passing Hungarian soldiers. Jackson asked Sony to build nine enormous steel-and-fiberglass statues of himself, which were placed in European cities in the spring of 1995. *HIStory*'s cover uses the same image – metal-Michael stands before a sky on fire, rising above ruin and chaos around him.

The album, which would sell 20 million copies worldwide, remains an astonishing achievement in superstar narcissism. "When I think of that album cover, it just doesn't add up," says Wild. "That wasn't the guy I worked with for three years."

LOST IN CLUBLAND

Jackson battles his demons with a heavy dose of industrial funk on this revealing package of remixes. By Jon Dolan

WHEN NIRVANA'S "NEVERMIND" KNOCKED MICHAEL JACKSON'S *Dangerous* out of the Number One spot on the *Billboard* Hot 200 in 1992, it was hard to miss the symbolism: The raw power of grunge's first superstars had instantly made the King of Pop feel obsolete. But when *Blood on the Dance Floor* came out five years later, close listeners picked up on something surprising: Michael had clearly found inspiration in the Alternative Nation. The disc, eight club remixes of songs from *HIStory* and five new tracks, is Jackson's weirdest, most abrasive and – arguably – most revealing record. The new tunes are primarily intense, industrial-funk dirges that provide a vivid snapshot of his contorted psyche at the time. (Engineer Rob Hoffman, who worked on the record, recalls that

Nine Inch Nails' *The Downward Spiral* was a key influence.) On the gnashing, hissing, Michael-penned "Morphine," he takes on the perspective of the drug, a dealer-doctor and just-say-no scolds, singing "Demerol/Oh, God, he's taking Demerol," alluding to an opiate he was allegedly addicted to. Over the operatic goth-soul of "Is It Scary," he sings, "I'll be grotesque before your eyes." It's the sound of a man doing battle with the voices in his head.

Despite the limited amount of new material on the disc, it was produced with the same excess that had marked every Jackson album since *Thriller*. When Slash – no stranger to studio bombast – arrived to cut some guitar parts, he was stunned by what he encountered. "I never saw him once during those sessions," the Guns n' Roses guitarist recalls. "He had more than two studios active with guys working on stuff. Finally I'd find a producer, and the producer would be like, 'Fuck, I don't know what's going on, I didn't even know you were part of the project.' That was when I started to see just how haphazard the whole Michael Jackson empire was."

When the call for remix submissions came in from Jackson HQ, the remixers (including house-music legend Todd Terry) reacted as if they'd won the lottery. Lauryn Hill said she "screamed like a woman" when Jackson contacted the Fugees in the studio. The group ended up having a more hands-on MJ experience than Slash did.

"I played him some stuff," says Wyclef Jean, who added booming snare drums, a "Beat It" sample and a rap from John Forté to "2 Bad." "He did all of the rhythms in his mouth and his feet, and those ended up being the exact rhythms you hear on the record. He was talking about Jamaica, how, when he was young, he went to Jamaica, and he said I reminded him of somebody in Jamaica with the long hair. I was like 'Oh, are you talking about Bob Marley?' He was like 'Yeah!'"

Blood ended up being the bestselling remix disc ever, and has gone on to sell more than 6 million copies. At this point, MJ was breaking records no one cared about. Well, no one except Wyclef. "Michael owes me money," he said a decade after the album came out. "Mike, holler at me!"

BACK IN THE GROOVE

On his final album, Michael got fresh and
funky again, concocting a sumptuous collection
of lush R&B, with guest shots by everyone
from Biggie to Rod Serling. By Jon Dolan

LUSCIOUS JACKSON
*Released in 2001,
"Invincible" was his first
album of all-new tracks
in a decade.*

IT WAS A BEAUTIFUL NEW YORK MORNING, AND MICHAEL JACKSON NEEDED SOME fresh air. Rodney Jerkins, who'd been working long hours with Jackson on his forthcoming album, called the singer in his hotel room and told him to get dressed. "Are you going to get in touch with security?" Jackson asked. "No," Jerkins replied. "You're going to get in my car." ★ They drove through the city all day. "We went to Harlem, through Manhattan. People were looking like…what?" Jerkins recalls. "I took him to the Virgin Megastore to buy CDs and DVDs. People went crazy! I wanted him to see that it's not all about going to the studio. I wanted him to see creativity comes from having fun." ★ *Invincible*, Jackson's last record, was an attempt to put Peter Pan back under the bed and return to the sonically lush R&B of his youth, updated for the 21st century. Jackson talked about a "return to love"

and wanting sounds that were "funky" and "fresh." "The goal was always to get him dancing," says keyboardist-arranger Brad Buxer. "He better be dancing. If he did, you knew you were going in the right direction."

To outsiders, Jackson often seemed totally sealed off. Colleagues and collaborators insist he kept a watchful eye on the music world. "I'd mention a song, and he would know the song and sing the chorus," recalls LA Reid. "He was very in tune with the contemporary landscape."

Younger collaborators were similarly impressed by his enthusiasm. "When I got there, I was thinking to myself, 'Where's Bubbles the chimp? Where's the hyperbaric chamber?'" recalls Teron Beal, who co-wrote "Heaven Can Wait," one of the album's ballads. "I didn't see any of that. He'd introduce himself to delivery guys, anyone who came through. He'd be listening to a track – loud! – and I'd see the back of his head bobbing, then he'd start snapping his neck. I was like, 'Oh, shit, this is a 40-year-old black man from Gary, Indiana. This guy's a pimp!'"

Jackson hoped Dr. Dre would produce the album, but the hip-hop legend turned him down. "I like working with new artists or people that I've worked with in the past," Dre said. "All I have to do is go in the studio, and basically they're going to bust their ass." So Jackson reached out instead to old friends like Teddy Riley, who had been working with him since *Dangerous*, and R. Kelly, who wrote *HIStory*'s "You Are Not Alone." Jerkins was the newest, and at that point, hottest of the crew. His signature airy melodies and fluttery beats had shaped hits like Destiny's Child's "Say My Name" and Brandy and Monica's "The Boy Is Mine." "When we started doing demos, I'd have a call with him every night at 3 or 4 a.m.," recalls Jerkins. "He was in Germany or New York, and I'd play him stuff, and he'd make suggestions. As we continued the touch-ups, he got more involved."

Jerkins' first batch of demos consisted of 60 songs, all laid down in one month. "He wanted something new," Jerkins says. "I told him, 'We can do that, but we're going to need some of the old-school elements.' I wanted to bring that *Off the Wall* sound." That sound was evident in "You Rock My World," which would become the album's first single and its lone hit. Jackson sings

with more funk finesse than he has in ages, gelling perfectly with disco strings, lush harmonies and a sumptuous groove.

"Privacy," a taut R&B jam, featured an anti-paparazzi rant and a percussion sound created when one of Jerkins' engineers smashed a light bulb with a stick. Jackson had other interesting conceptual ideas. "Unbreakable" includes a from-beyond-the-grave freestyle by the Notorious B.I.G., taken from a 1996 performance. For "Threatened," a creepy stalker-themed jam, Jackson had an even more adventurous idea for a cameo. "He said, 'We need a voice like that guy on *The Twilight Zone*, Rod Serling,'" Jerkins says. "'Get him.'" Serling died in 1975, so Jerkins spent dozens of hours watching *Twilight Zone* DVDs, searching for phrases that could be hewn into a voice-over ("If he said 'I hate ya' and 'nature,' anything that could fit together"), then constructed a Serling monologue using Pro Tools. "It was the most nerve-racking, tiresome thing I've ever done in my life," he says. "But it was amazing to get it right."

Jackson's own vocals took a similarly tortuous path. Given the task of punching up a few lines in a verse, he'd conference-call his vocal coach, Seth Riggs, and do scales for two hours. To get psyched to sing his parts, he'd dance to a song's backing track for as long as seven minutes.

One of the songs in which Jackson's athletelike training regimen paid off was "Butterflies," a spare soul plea where his voice strives to hit high notes he likely hadn't attempted since puberty. "We originally demoed it with a woman singing – Marsha Ambrosius of Floetry," says Vidal Davis, who helped produce the song. "So it was hard for him to hit those notes. We did tons and tons of takes. We sampled his fingers snapping for the beat. He has the loudest finger snaps in the world."

As *Invincible* took shape, classic elements of a Michael Jackson album fell into place. Carlos Santana soloed on the Latin-flavored Riley joint "Whatever Happens," giving the album its requisite superstar-guitarist spot. R. Kelly sent in a gospel-tinged "change the world" entreaty, "Cry," in which Jackson asks humanity to join him in a worldwide mass sob. And, of course, there were Jackson's own outrageously sweep-

TAKING IT TO THE STREETS
*Jackson promotes "Invincible" outside the Virgin
Megastore in New York's Times Square at his
first-ever in-store appearance, November 2001.*

ing creations. "Speechless" was an ode to the power of love that Jackson wrote while sitting in a tree in his yard at Neverland Ranch.

"The Lost Children" was even more grandiose, with Jackson the only songwriter credited on the track, which features a children's choir conducted by Tom Bahler, who'd arranged vocals for "We Are the World," and a spoken interlude from Jackson's son Prince Michael. "This one's for all the lost children/Wishing them well and wishing them home," Jackson sings.

As *Invincible* neared completion, Jackson refused to turn it in to the label; songs were mixed 17 times, he redid his vocals seven times, even if everyone agreed he'd nailed it on the first. Eventually, the cost approached $30 million. Sony president Tommy Mottola's patience was wearing thin. "We were in the cross hairs," engineer Bruce Swedien recalls. "At one meeting, Tommy started yelling at everyone, 'Finish the goddamn record!'"

Tensions escalated when *Invincible* was finally completed in the fall of 2001. To promote the album, Sony staged an all-star concert that September at Madison Square Garden, pegged to the 30th anniversary of Jackson's debut as a solo artist, where he appeared onstage with his brothers for the first time since the 1984 *Victory* tour. "You Rock My World" was a hit, but it was clear by early 2002 that *Invincible* wasn't going to be the career reinvention that Jackson hoped for. Jackson blamed Sony, going so far as to call Mottola a racist and staging rallies across Manhattan against his own label. "He's very, very devilish," Jackson said.

The persecution fantasy gave Jackson an excuse for the inconceivable: Rather than selling 100 million, *Invincible* barely reached 2 million. But Jackson told Jerkins not to worry, that the genius of what they'd done would eventually be recognized. "Someday," he said, "it's going to see the light of day."

BLACK SUPER HERO

African-American artists and intellectuals, from Jay-Z to Henry Louis Gates, weigh in on Jackson's legacy. By Touré

WHEN MICHAEL JACKSON WAS A BOY, YOU DIDN'T HAVE TO SAY "BLACK is beautiful," you just had to look at him and you knew. In 1969, as black people were getting comfortable with the idea that African features are gorgeous, he arrived as the perfect punctuation of that idea. He was cherubic with his rich brown skin, a broad nose and a big halo of curls atop his head at a time when the Afro was a powerful symbol of black pride. "People responded viscerally to Michael Jackson's beauty," says Henry Louis Gates Jr., the Harvard professor. 1969 was a year after the assassination of Dr. Martin Luther King Jr., a time when the black-power and civil rights movements seemed to be disintegrating, but Michael showed up, a soul-music prodigy irrepressibly optimistic and bursting with youthful enthusiasm. "Here was a child who clearly understood the R&B idiom," says music-industry veteran Gary Harris. "He was some sort of test-tube creation from a mad soul doctor's lab. If Diana Ross and Stevie Wonder had a child, it would have been Michael Jackson."

BLACK IS BEAUTIFUL
Michael with full Afro in 1978.

"You had people in France, South America imitating a black kid from Gary, Indiana," some of those people in Iowa grew, they we because they got comfortable imitating a

He quickly became the number-one black child star of his era, and of all time. The first four Jackson 5 singles each topped *Billboard*'s Hot 100, an unbelievable start. Black people fell in love so hard, he became more than an artist – he became a member of the family. You didn't want anything to happen to him so much that you felt protective the way you did about a younger brother. "He was ours," says the rapper Q-Tip. "He meant everything to black culture."

It wasn't just about Michael. A few years after the Johnson administration declared the black family broken with the Moynihan Report, the Jackson family was large, intact, vibrant, successful and seemingly happy, giving America an idealized image of domestic bliss. Jay-Z told me he grew up pretending to be Michael, singing alongside his two older sisters and brother. "Here you had Michael and four brothers," says the Rev. Al Sharpton, "all talented and all cute, and the strong father and the mother who was matriarchal and Janet, and it was like, 'Wow, all this talent in this family, showing we could do something.' We were proud of that."

Michael had a second family: Motown was a deeply trusted brand in millions of black households. If Berry Gordy said it was good enough to release, you could bet it was great. The Jackson 5 were the last great act to come out of the Detroit label, further proof of Malcolm Gladwell's theory in *Outliers: The Story of Success* that life timing is critical to success, that the historical forces swirling around the moment when you emerge can make all the difference. "The Jacksons were the first family in line to truly benefit from the post-civil-rights era with America's new open-arms policy toward black entertainment," says ?uestlove of the Roots. "1969 was the year the social floodgates opened, and an 11-year-old led the charge in post-Malcolm/Martin/Motown America. Historians always forget the third-most-important 'M' to help black America get access to the promised land is Motown."

Thriller came out at the end of 1982, as the affirmative-action generation was beginning to make its move. Jesse Jackson would make a bid for the presidency, Eddie Murphy would launch his assault on the top layers of Hollywood,

Oprah Winfrey would start her legendary talk show, and Bill Cosby would create the best-rated sitcom of the decade. Even before all that started, the vibe of black ascensionism was in the air, and Michael saw no reason why race should hold him back from the most elite level of his profession. He decided to ride his excellence to the zenith. Current Motown president Sylvia Rhone says, "Throughout his career, his success dramatically affected my view of what was possible and open for African-Americans."

Many blacks now compare Michael with Barack Obama – perhaps the highest possible compliment in black America. Not only are they both integrationists and racial harmonists, but they both were determined to reach the top while refusing to let race hold them back. "There's so many components of why Barack Obama is president," says Sean "Diddy" Combs, "and Michael Jackson is one of them. He started a change in the perception of the African-American male on a worldwide level: his strength, always putting himself in a power position, being seen as a hero." Sharpton echoes the point. "Way before Tiger Woods or Barack Obama, Michael made black people go pop-culture global," he says. "You had people in France, South America and Iowa comfortable with their kids imitating a black kid from Gary, Indiana. And when some of those people in Iowa grew, they were comfortable with voting for Barack Obama because they got comfortable imitating a black kid named Michael Jackson when they were young. Obama is a phenomenon, but he's the result of a process that Michael helped America graduate to."

Michael was also a boardroom killer. In the decades before him, black recording artists were, as James Brown observed, in the show but not in show business. Many ended up losing the copyrights to their own songs and pocketing a fraction of the money their music brought in. Jackson knew all about that history. "He knew Berry Gordy made his money off copyrights," cultural critic Nelson George says. "He knew the value of songs. That's something he understood." In 1984, when the ATV music-publishing catalog, which contained 251 Beatles songs, including "Yesterday," "Let It Be" and "Hey Jude," as well as work from Bob Dylan, went up for sale, Jackson went

and Iowa comfortable with their kids says the Rev. Al Sharpton. "And when re comfortable voting for Barack Obama black kid named Michael Jackson."

after it. After 10 months of negotiation, Jackson purchased the catalog for $47.5 million. His stake is now worth more than 10 times that, and the move was easily his shrewdest business conquest – and the asset that kept him afloat during his financially troubled last years. It proved his savvy, separating him from all those previous black artists who lacked the power to control the music business. But more than that, the symbolic power of Jackson owning the Beatles' music cannot be overstated. Not only did he become as big as the Beatles, he *bought* them too. A century after American whites owned blacks, a black performer owned the product of the most elite white group in the world. It was an amazing turnabout, and one blacks took special pride in. A few nights after Jackson died, I was in L.A., searching the radio for an MJ song, when I came across "Strawberry Fields Forever" on an oldies station. I said, "Fuck it, Mike owns this. Same difference." And I listened.

By the Nineties, Jackson no longer looked like a black person – after a series of surgeries, his facial features and skin color had become more and more Caucasoid. "I don't think there was any question: There was disquiet in the black community about the color thing," says George. "It was an issue. People didn't wanna go out and say, 'He's fuckin' becoming white,' but people were like, 'What's that about?'" As Jackson was literally assimilating, we struggled with his choices but never symbolically tossed him out of the race, even though he seemed to be trying to surgically remove himself from it. "The reason black folk never turned their backs on him," says Georgetown professor Michael Eric Dyson, "is because we realized he was merely acting out on his face what we collectively have been tempted to do in our souls: whitewash the memory and trace of our offending blackness." Still, we struggled to understand why. Some have said he no longer wanted to see his father in the mirror, but there seem to be deeper forces at play.

"I think he wanted to be a symbol of universalism," Gates says, "and he erroneously thought his skin color, hair texture, the length of his nose and shape of his chin inhibited that. You could say he was appealing to the universal, but there's no way of escaping, even giving him the benefit of the doubt, that it's

a function of Negro self-hatred and self-loathing, which is a function of slavery, Jim Crow, segregation and racism, which made blacks hate the very things that make them beautiful."

Those who knew Jackson well say he wasn't trying to surgically remove himself from the race. Producer Teddy Riley, who worked on Jackson's album *Dangerous*, says, "Of course he loved being black. We'd be in sessions where we'd just vibe out and he'd say, 'We are black, and we are the most talented people on the face of the Earth.' I know this man loved his culture, he loved his race, he loved his people."

"As a fellow child of a taskmaster, no one knows self-distorted insecurity like I do," says ?uestlove. "A person ashamed of his roots would never have made a gazillion odes to Africa as he's done." And even as his face got whiter, his music stayed black and rooted in the R&B tradition he mastered as a kid.

The day he died, it seemed something on this realm changed. "When I got the news," the rapper Nas says, "the weather around me immediately changed drastically. It suddenly rained so hard. Wind blew like crazy. Clouds did something different. It was as if you felt him leaving the world." People struggled to wrap their heads around the magnitude of his death. "This is the biggest loss since, dare I say, Martin Luther King," says Q-Tip. "He moved the culture that much. He moved the needles that much."

Now that he's gone, everything Wacko Jacko has been rightly hushed, and everything that made him the King of Pop has taken over the mind space he fills. "When you have a body of work that great, it's not about you personally," former Motown CEO Andre Harrell says. "It's about your body of work. We're not gonna concentrate on the negative, we're gonna deal with the music. It took his death to get all the personal stuff out of the way and really get back to the reason why we're interested in loving him." In death, his songs have been liberated from his eccentricities like ghosts released from a haunted mansion, free again to fly through the air and spread joy. And because the music business can no longer create a star as big as he was at his height, it seems likely that he'll be the King of Pop forever.

SHOW TIME

Pop's greatest performer launched some of the biggest tours of all time. From the Jackson 5 on the chitlin circuit to rehearsals for This Is It, a complete guide. By Douglas Wolk

THE EARLY YEARS

1967 - 79

Even before Michael, Marlon, Jermaine, Tito and Jackie Jackson called themselves the Jackson 5, they were winning talent contests in their native Gary, Indiana. By 1967, the group hit the road, playing the all-black "chitlin circuit" and opening for acts from the Temptations to Sam and Dave. In August of that year, the Jacksons won the amateur contest at Harlem's famed Apollo Theater.

TASKMASTER "We're gonna make a lot of money, boys," father Joe Jackson told his young sons, whom he rehearsed mercilessly: He reportedly slapped Michael for missing dance steps and would routinely hold a whip in his hand while they practiced.

HIGHER GROUND After signing to Motown, the Jackson 5 became almost instant superstars, facing Beatlemania levels of hysteria at their shows – which hit arenas and stadiums as early as 1970. An August 1971 show at New York's Madison Square Garden had to be stopped two minutes after it started when fans rushed the stage.

AROUND THE WORLD The Jackson 5's fame soon spread globally – they toured the U.K. and Europe in 1972, starting with a private performance for the queen of England, which Michael would later call "one of the greatest honors of my life." In 1973, they hit Japan. They toured the world throughout the 1970s, even hitting Senegal in 1974.

DISCO FEVER
*Jackson at the Forum
in Los Angeles, 1974*

TRIUMPH

JULY - SEPTEMBER 1981

Triumph was officially a Jacksons tour, but for the first time, Michael was clearly the star of the show rather than just the frontman – the show had five songs from *Off the Wall*, as well as his 1972 solo hit "Ben." In a sign of stunts to come, Jackson used a magic trick designed by Doug Henning to disappear in a cloud of smoke.

SUPERSIZE ME Only a few years earlier, the Jacksons – struggling to draw crowds that perceived them as an oldies act – were touring in Winnebagos; now they closed the *Triumph* tour with four sold-out nights at the Los Angeles Forum. "The stage got bigger, the show was longer, the dance moves got more elaborate," recalls touring drummer Jonathan Moffett. "All of it had grown, and I was 10 feet up on a drum riser for the first time in my life."

CRYING WOLF Michael claimed it was the last time he would go on tour – not the last time he'd repeat that particular threat. "We've been around the world twice, performed before kings and ambassadors," he said. "It's time to move on."

SHOWSTOPPER "She's Out of My Life" found Michael crying onstage most nights, a trick he'd repeat on the next few tours.

SHAKE YOUR BODY
Michael and his brothers on the "Triumph" tour, 1981.

VICTORY

JULY - DECEMBER 1984

He tried to get out, but they kept pulling him back in: Michael had just become a solo superstar with *Thriller,* but his family pressured him into one more group tour. Nevertheless, Michael took creative control, drawing storyboards for an elaborate spectacle that kicked off with Muppet-ish monsters battling a knight who pulls a sword from a stone.

SET LIST Though the show took its name from the Jacksons' 1984 album, the set list ignored its songs entirely, instead focusing on Michael's solo work – "Beat It" and "Billie Jean" were highlights.

CONTROVERSY Promoted by Don King, the *Victory* tour drew criticism for high ticket prices ($30 a seat) – and a buying procedure that required postal money orders. Michael responded to the controversy by donating his share of the profits to charity. The tour grossed $81 million, a figure exceeded at the time only by Bruce Springsteen's *Born in the U.S.A.* tour.

GRAND ENDING At the final stop of the tour, Jackson shocked his brothers by announcing, "This is our last and final show." He didn't perform with them again until 2001.

FLASHING LIGHTS
Michael and his brothers open a 1984 "Victory" tour show with "Wanna Be Startin' Somethin'."

BAD

Jackson's first solo tour featured illusions designed by Siegfried and Roy (he'd disappear from one side of the stage and reappear on the other), and a troupe of dancers who mimicked his videos' choreography. In his silver-studded, heavily buckled stage outfit, Jackson projected a more adult sexuality, punctuating his dancing with frequent crotch grabs. With $125 million in ticket sales, *Bad* was the highest-grossing tour ever at the time.

PRINCESS DIARY At a show at London's Wembley Stadium, Prince Charles sent a message backstage asking Michael to skip "Dirty Diana." But 10 minutes later, Princess Diana arrived in person, telling Jackson, "I want you to sing that song like you've never sung it before."

STARTING OVER Jackson's perfectionism was in high gear: One day in rehearsals, he heard a wrong note, recalls assistant music director Kevin Dorsey. "He said, 'Let's go from the top.' I thought he meant the top of the song – he meant the top of the show!"

SHOWSTOPPER "I Just Can't Stop Loving You" was performed as a duet with then-unknown backup singer Sheryl Crow.

BIGGER AND BADDER
Jackson in Kansas City's Kemper Arena, February 1988, on the "Bad" tour.

DANGEROUS

JUNE - OCTOBER
AND DECEMBER 1992

AUGUST - NOVEMBER 1993

In a sign of career decline, this tour avoided the U.S., hitting Europe, Asia, South America and Mexico instead. Jackson, who faced his first child-molestation charges during the tour, ended up cutting it short and checking into a London rehab clinic for painkiller addiction.

BLOOD ON THE DANCE FLOOR Even early on, Jackson was showing signs that the tour was overstraining him. "Two days a week was a good workout for Michael," says assistant music director Kevin Dorsey. "And on *Dangerous*, they started pushing that to three or four sometimes. There was just no way you can expend that kind of energy for a two-and-a-half-hour show, back to back, 10 times. It's impossible."

GUNS N' JACKO Slash turned up to play guitar on "Black or White" at a couple of shows.

WORLD PARTY Jackson was joined by a chorus of children every night during "Heal the World," which also featured a giant inflatable globe.

LIFTOFF During "Man in the Mirror," Jackson donned a spacesuit and helmet. Then he – or a stuntman who took his place midsong – would strap on a jet pack and fly out of the stadium. "He had to fly," keyboardist Greg Phillinganes says. "I remember seeing the faces in the crowd, and they were mesmerized. It was such a beautiful thing."

HISTORY

SEPTEMBER 1996 - JANUARY 1997; MAY - OCTOBER 1997

By this point, Jackson was fully into his decadent phase, from his gold Versace outfit to the onstage scrims and statues that represented the "Temple of History." In Prague, a 35-foot statue of Jackson appeared on a platform that had been used for the city's Stalin monument. "It was the talk, all over Europe, that Stalin had come down and Michael had gone up," recalls drummer Jonathan Moffett. Guitarist Jennifer Batten calls *HIStory* the least favorite of her three Jackson tours, "because

I'd played most of the tunes before already and had to wear a ghastly S&M-looking costume."

SPACE ODDITY The show began with a spaceship that crashed into the stage. A robotic figure emerged and took off its helmet, revealing Jackson's face.

CHINESE DEMOCRACY Jackson invoked the Tiananmen Square showdown in "Earth Song," facing down a tank.

THIS IS IT

SCHEDULED JULY 2009 - MARCH 2010

He was determined to put on the greatest show on Earth, including 20-foot-tall puppets and a *Thriller* segment featuring 3-D footage. There was also an ecological theme, what director Kenny Ortega calls "a deep green statement – [Michael] wanted to not only entertain but to get those messages across."

FAMILY MAN In addition to earning some much-needed cash, Jackson was eager for his young children to see him perform for the first time. "They were now old enough to appreciate what he did," says Ortega.

ENDLESS HIGHWAY One musician who signed up for the 50 London shows was told that it could go on for three years or more, with extended engagements around the world.

MICHAEL LIVES ON Sony Pictures bid $60 million to release a movie from HD footage of the rehearsals.

A NEW KIND OF HOLLYWOOD MUSICAL

With 'Billie Jean,' Jackson perfected the video, but he never stopped trying to take it further. By Rob Sheffield

EVERYTHING THAT MADE MICHAEL JACKSON THE ULTIMATE VIDEO star is right there in "Billie Jean." It's a simple production: no other dancers, no choir, just MJ alone with his music, twitching like all the demons in the song are battling to burst out of his skinny body. He hops on his toes, spins, kicks, pops his leather collar. He's a master of physical grace, but you can also see he's a scared kid, a little dazed by his own glare, tormented by the rush of music surging through him when he'd rather sit under a tree with a good book somewhere quiet. Somewhere safe. Somewhere he won't get, no matter how far he runs into the night.

"Billie Jean" defined Jackson as a video performer, but he made all kinds of videos over the years: sexy dance clips, old-time Hollywood production numbers, big-budget monstrosities. Once he perfected the form, he kept messing with it, hyping his videos into showbiz events full of guest stars, spoken-word interludes, special effects, sometimes leaving the song behind completely. He couldn't help exposing himself on camera, revealing his most attractive traits, as well as his most appalling, indulging every whim. Was there anybody in his entourage who had the clout to say, "Yo, Mike, maybe this song doesn't need a 20-minute CGI epic where you run through the burning forest rescuing orphans?" Probably not. But everything Jackson had to say was there in his dazzling body language.

He wasn't the first pop star who could dance, but he was the one who defined the pop star as dancer. Donna Summer was the queen of disco, but nobody noticed her moves, much less tried to steal them. Yet after "Billie Jean," dancing was part of the job description, and every dead-ass klutz with a hit felt compelled to bust a move in public, because that's how Michael did it. Even Whitney. Even Lionel. Hell, even Bruce.

He loved the Old Hollywood dream factory, the film-noir hats and the *West Side Story*-style gang dances. There's as much Montgomery Clift in his videos as James Brown or Mick Jagger, as he escapes into a Fifties/Eighties fantasy where the 1960s never happened, where nobody's heard of the Beatles – or of the Jackson 5, for that matter.

Michael Jackson defined the video as an art form; he also defined it as a symbol of megalomaniacal excess. Sometimes both at the same time.

168

DANCE ON THE FLOOR
Jackson's video for "Billie Jean" became an MTV smash and introduced him to a whole new audience.

"Don't Stop 'Til You Get Enough"
1979
**Before the dawn of MTV, Michael put on a tux
and danced all by his lonesome**

This video captures Michael the way the world fell in love with him: the boy next door living out his glammiest disco dreams, putting on a tux and strutting his stuff. You can't help getting swept away by his joy and exuberance. You also can't help noticing he's alone – the girl he's singing to is nowhere in sight. All his best dance performances were solo flights; it was as if his desires (and his beauty) were too intense to be shared with flesh-and-blood human beings, and he needed to protect us because we'd go up in flames if we got too close.

"Billie Jean"
1983
**After the video reinvented MTV, Michael took over the world
with his live performance on the 'Motown 25' special**

You always hear that MJ broke the color line on MTV, and the fact that it's wildly inaccurate may be beside the point. In 1981 and 1982, MTV played lots of black artists, as long as they fit into ideas of conventional rock mythology: Joan Armatrading, Gary "U.S." Bonds, the Bus Boys, Tina Turner, even Prince. What MTV originally wouldn't touch – and what MJ refused to play down – was disco. But his disco was so expansive that there was no way to resist. And as far as MTV's audience was concerned, Michael Jackson arrived just in time to rule a kingdom he had helped create. The mysterioso night-town vibe of the video was the perfect backdrop as Jackson acted out all the sexy dread in the song, showing off his ungodly collection of kicks and zooms and spins.

He took the song in a different direction in his most famous live TV performance, on the *Motown 25* special. The show should have been no big deal – all MJ had to do was lip-sync a song that had already been a hit for months by the time the special aired. After a medley of Jackson 5 hits, he shooed his bros offstage, the way he must have always wanted. "I like those songs a lot," he said. "But especially, I like the *new* songs." And for the next five minutes, he showed how new a song could be.

MJ knew how to rule a stage – but as a longtime TV pro, he also knew what worked on the small screen. Tonight, he did everything that worked, with dance moves that merited a Nobel Prize in Physics: tossing his fedora aside, miming a pimp-rageous hair-comb move, pumping his long, elastic thighs, leaning hard on his knees to create an unbearable sense of anticipation. He seemed to stop and restart time at will, flaunting his athletic power and speed, yet oddly friendly and gentle, even slipping his hand into his pocket for a mock-casual look. Then he took off on his historic three-second moonwalk. We'd never seen him do his thing in front of other people, and it was a weirdly uncharacteristic emotional triumph for this loneliest of performers. Lots of dancers had done the moonwalk before. But not while singing a song like "Billie Jean." It was like seeing Jordan sink a three-pointer while playing Hamlet.

MICHAEL'S MOMENT
On the "Motown 25" TV special, Jackson sang "Billie Jean" and introduced his moonwalk to the world.

TOUGH ENOUGH
To match the hard-rock feel of "Beat It," Jackson and director Bob Giraldi created a video that matched a gritty story line with elaborate, "West Side Story"-style group choreography.

"Beat It"
1983
Michael's powers are strong enough to turn gang toughs into Broadway dancers

The lonely spaceboy boldly leaves his solitary room to go into the big, bad world outside, with nothing to protect him except the fact that his dance moves have the power to stop gang wars. The video celebrates his androgyny ("Don't wanna see no blood, don't be a macho man," sneered the world's most famous male – a shocking line then and now), blending gay disco and straight-boy metal into a fantasy of free-floating night-world eros. Michael was proud of the fact that there were actual tough kids in the video, although not as tough as they seemed: "We fed them during breaks," he wrote, "and they all cleaned up and put their trays away." Maybe that's why when Michael shows up in the middle of the rumble and busts a few moves, before you know it, all the gangsters are hypnotized by the Jedi mind power of his hips. The dancing gets downright sloppy at the end, as the leather boys try to cop his moves while Michael floats right past them. Morrissey would have eaten his cats to make this video.

"Thriller"
1983
Not really a music video but a short film about dancing zombies

For people who looked down on music videos, this was a classy project that redeemed the genre. For people who just liked watching Michael Jackson move, it was a Hollywood zombie movie – handled by a real Hollywood director, John Landis of *Animal House* fame – with a few minutes of music thrown in. Landis suggested that they simultaneously make a documentary, *Making Michael Jackson's "Thriller,"* to help defray the costs of the video's $500,000 budget. The making-of video became the bestselling music videocassette of all time, and slumber parties everywhere re-created the zombie dance. MTV premiered this with a weekend where it played every hour on the hour – and it's 14 minutes long. Best moment: Werecat Michael confesses to his girl, portrayed by *Playboy* centerfold Ola Ray, "I'm not like other guys."

"Say Say Say"
1983
As a couple of snake-oil salesmen, Paul McCartney and Michael try to be lovable rascals

After helming the mind-blowing "Beat It," director Bob Giraldi grandly declared, "There's only one star on my sets, and that's me." Then he made "Say Say Say" and proved it takes more than a clever director and a vast budget to make a decent video. Paul McCartney and Michael Jackson's cute-off was enough to put this barely even existent song at Number One for six weeks. But all the fancy costumes, expensive sets and corny gags look incredibly dumb, like a dress rehearsal for *Give My Regards to Broad Street.* The only great moment comes when Michael tries to romance a young lady who looks just like him – every high school cafeteria in America buzzed with the rumor that the girl was secretly Michael in drag. It was really only La Toya.

"Bad"
1987
Continuing to try to top himself, Jackson brought in Martin Scorsese for this 18-minute video

It had been a while since Michael had hit the screen – two years since "We Are the World," where he was still the fragile young *Thriller* boy-child. Now he looked barely recognizable, pushing 30 in a full-body leather fetish suit and a radically re-sculpted face. Prancing through a Brooklyn G-train station screeching, "Who's bad?" yet not actually doing anything bad except a little spray-painting on the wall, accompanied by a Chippendales chorus line of the least ominous gangstas in history – it was a different look, to say the least. With a script from Richard Price and direction from Martin Scorsese, this was an ambitious long-form video that actually worked, thanks to Michael's deft performance as the prep-school kid and Wesley Snipes' mugging as his ghetto nemesis. But in a way, it was the end. From then on, MJ would no longer be content to make music videos – he kept trying to transcend the form with mini-movies, ending up with productions too overstuffed for the TV screen but too small for anywhere else.

WHO'S BAD?
*Jackson and Scorsese shot the "Bad"
video at a Brooklyn subway stop.*

MICHAEL, ARE YOU OK?
The "Smooth Criminal" video was a nearly 10-minute segment drawn from Jackson's 1989 film "Moonwalker."

"Smooth Criminal"
1988
*Michael surrounds himself with gangsters,
who try in vain to lean like him*

The big difference between the "Thriller" and "Bad" videos: Now Michael was relying on group choreography, so instead of wondering how the hell he could make his lean body moonwalk, you wondered whether all those "Smooth Criminal" pachucos in the zoot suits were really leaning sideways. They weren't – it was wires and harnesses, although Michael wore special anti-gravity shoes for live performances. (Michael patented the shoes in 1993, but the patent expired in 2005 when he failed to pay the required maintenance fee.) And he was seething with adult sexual hostility, which made him less attractive: In "The Way You Make Me Feel," as in "Thriller," he followed a girl down the street trying to catch her eye, but now he just seemed like one of the bullies from the "Beat It" video. "Smooth Criminal" expresses the same bile, but in a flashier, more stylized way, as Michael shoots up the saloon with a vintage Tommy gun. It's like a clash between a Desi Arnaz mambo party and one of those 1940s Havana crime flicks. And Michael's white suit really did look awesome. The version commonly seen on MTV was only a small part of the show; the *Moonwalker* film had a considerably expanded version featuring Joe Pesci as Mr. Big.

"Man in the Mirror"
1988
*Going for inspiration, Michael inexplicably made
a video with almost no Michael*

You'd never know it from this clip, but Michael gave one of his most amazing performances doing this song at the 1988 Grammys with a gospel choir. This video? A dumb montage of tearjerker news clips, apparently slapped together at random. Martin Luther King Jr., Gandhi, Hitler, JFK, RFK, Lech Walesa, sickly-looking children in USA FOR AFRICA shirts – it looks like an infomercial for the Heal the Kittens With Jesus Juice Foundation. By the time Mother Teresa shows up, the video has killed off the song – no human warmth, just a superstar windbag scolding people for not taking him seriously enough.

"Liberian Girl"
1989
*Overloaded with minor celebs from Corey Feldman
to pre-'Idol' Paula Abdul*

Some people praise clips like "Leave Me Alone" for supposedly showing Michael's edginess, self-awareness or (crikey, are you kidding?) sense of humor. But as a statement on jaded stardom, "Liberian Girl" is more ridiculous, and therefore better. Michael puffs up this epic with a huge cast of celebrities, minor stars, D-listers and Corey Feldman, showing off how much money he's spending because that's all he has to say. Isn't that Paula Abdul? Lou Ferrigno? Lord, it's Olivia Newton-John! This was never a hit and never got any airplay at the time, but it remains a monument to Michael's egomania at its most harmless.

"Black or White"
1991
*A heartfelt plea for racial harmony, followed by
crotch-grabbing and car-smashing*

That Macaulay Culkin – he sure can rap! This classic had all the signs of a typical hyped-to-death Michael Jackson video extravaganza, with fans everywhere tuning in to watch the Sunday-night debut after *The Simpsons*. It was lighter and more fun than any *Bad* video, maybe because Michael was back to solo dancing, pleading for racial harmony by twirling through a hilarious EPCOT-style series of international locales. (Hey, we're in Russia! Wait, is this China? Those are pagodas, right?)

Another John Landis-directed epic, "Black or White" begins with Culkin using his guitar to blast George Wendt out of his La-Z-Boy into the sky. But the big controversy concerned the extremely strange ending: Michael prowls the streets of the city, smashing car windows, grabbing his crotch and screaming for vengeance. After his sensitive plea for universal love and brotherhood, it was a shock to see him turn into a late-night urban road warrior. The violent coda was never aired again. The short version ends with a gallery of faces morphing together, but the face you wind up remembering is Michael's. His charm, charisma and finger-popping vigor had returned in full force, and his future, for maybe the last time, looked virtually unlimited.

BEYOND COLOR
*The 11-minute "Black or White" video drew
criticism for its violent and sexually
suggestive closing sequence.*

"Remember the Time"
1992
Eddie Murphy and Magic Johnson guest-star, but Michael's kiss steals the show

An ancient Egyptian epic with Eddie Murphy as the pharaoh, supermodel Iman as his queen and Magic Johnson as the eunuch who bangs the gong, directed by the same guy who put Janet Jackson in a movie called *Poetic Justice*, where she plays a girl named Justice who likes poetry. It's a campy yet sentimental favorite from *Dangerous*, up there with the Herb Ritts-directed "In the Closet," where Michael loiters on a ranch in a tank top making eyes at Naomi Campbell. These songs pointed the way to the Grown-up Romantic Michael – including an awkward smooch with Iman – but like many of his futures, this never came to pass.

"You Are Not Alone"
1995
Then-wife Lisa Marie Presley goes topless, to no avail

Too bad John and Yoko had already claimed the title *Two Virgins*. Michael got naked with Lisa Marie, with soft-focus lighting that must have required Vaseline all over the lens. It was even more painful than their botched kiss at the 1994 MTV Video Music Awards, where Michael joked, "And they said it wouldn't last." The marriage survived for 20 months; this video seemed to go on slightly longer.

"Scream"
1995
Michael and Janet bond over their shared hatred of the media

At $7 million, this set the record as the most expensive video ever made, even though it's hard to see where all the money went. It's an elaborate tribute to *2001: A Space Odyssey*, and maybe also Jermaine's dusty "Bass Odyssey." Michael and Janet are stuck on their private silver spaceship, where they have some cute moments together: They cuddle up close, they play video games on the couch, they look like a couple of bored teenagers grounded for the weekend. The overall sense of bombast and hostility kept this from being much of a hit – how many times do you need to keep hearing this guy complain you don't appreciate him? But there's a moving sense of two lonely superstars craving a little human contact and reaching out to each other because nobody else could ever understand them.

Singing now looked physically painful for Michael, as he clenched his face into that zonked-out grimace that had become his only expression. There was no fun in this video, and that was the point; it couldn't have been further from the idea that a musical performance could be both scary and sexy, the way "Billie Jean" was.

The original video star had lost all his feel for TV dynamics. His movie-star-size ambitions made him unable to guess what worked on the small screen and what didn't. So he just got tinier as his special effects got bigger. He looked lost and desperate in bloated epics like "Earth Song" – but his chemistry with Janet makes "Scream" the last of his impressive video statements.

"You Rock My World"
2001
Even a Brando cameo couldn't save this from sinking without a trace

Marlon Brando? Chris Tucker? Michael Madsen? This attempt at a star-studded, big-budget, headline-grabbing comeback failed – or would have, if people had a chance to see how dismally it turned out. The gangster-movie motif was to "Smooth Criminal" what *Casino* was to *Goodfellas*. But hardly anyone noticed, even though the track crested to Number 10. He made one more video, for "Cry," but it consisted simply of a Hands Across America-style human chain without a trace of Michael.

It was the end of an era for Jackson – but also for the whole idea of music videos. By the time he unveiled "You Rock My World," MTV was barely playing any music at all. First, he perfected music videos, and then he attempted to transcend them; by the end, Michael Jackson had also outlived them.

WHAT WENT WRONG

He went from being the biggest star in the world to a reclusive, broken man – then his bid for a spectacular comeback was tragically cut short. The inside story of Jackson's fall and his final days. By Claire Hoffman and Brian Hiatt

MICHAEL JACKSON'S BODY LAY ON A METAL GURNEY in the county morgue in downtown Los Angeles. He was dressed in shiny black trousers, a thin hospital gown and nothing else. His feet were bare, his left arm scored with needle marks. His pale, narrow chest was covered in bruises – evidence of the medical efforts over the past few hours to save his life. Doctors and security guards milled in and out of the little room containing the gurney, eager to catch a glimpse of Jackson's body. ★ It had started late that Thursday morning, June 25th, 2009, when Jackson's own live-in doctor had tried frantically to revive him. By the time the medics arrived, responding to a desperate call to 911 at 12:21 p.m., they wanted to pronounce him dead on

FINAL FAREWELL
*From left: Jackie, R&B singer Usher,
Jermaine, Randy and Marlon
(bowing) at Jackson's memorial
service, July 7th, 2009, at the Staples
Center in Los Angeles.*

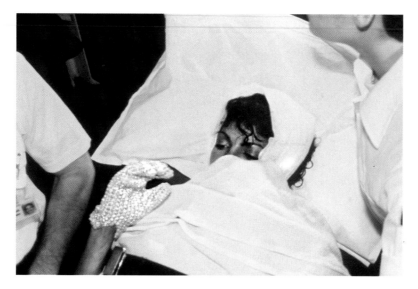

THE BEGINNING OF THE END

*Jackson's painkiller addiction has been traced back
to the incident when his hair caught fire while
filming a 1984 Pepsi commercial (above). Right: With
Macaulay Culkin (center) and friends in Bermuda,
1991. With his pet chimp Bubbles at Dodger Stadium,
1984. In a hyperbaric chamber, 1986.*

the spot. But Michael Jackson couldn't be dead. His body was lifted into the back of an ambulance and rushed to UCLA Medical Center, where a team of doctors worked for another hour, pounding defibrillator paddles on Jackson's chest, all of them hoping that they could keep one of music's greatest entertainers from ending up in this morgue.

Jackson's face, which he had so painfully reworked and concealed from the public for decades, now lay out in the open, undisguised under the morgue's harsh lights. The prosthesis he normally attached to his damaged nose was missing, revealing bits of cartilage surrounding a small, dark hole. But to those who passed through the room, Jackson's face looked porcelain, impeccable. After years of torment, Michael was finally at rest. "Seeing him lying there," recalls one eyewitness, "he looked peaceful."

Doctors would eventually perform two autopsies to try to understand why a thin, 50-year-old man who had danced for hours the night before would die so suddenly. The cause of death was ultimately ruled to be homicide from an overdose of the surgical anesthetic propofol, sold under the trade name Diprivan. Even as Jackson lay in the morgue on the afternoon of June 25th, detectives were already inside the singer's rented château in Bel-Air, gathering up the mother lode of prescription drugs that he kept on hand. The two large bags of medication investigators removed contained vials of Diprivan, which Jackson's physician, Dr. Conrad Murray, admitted to giving his client in the early hours of June 25th.

Within hours of Michael's death, La Toya Jackson and other members of the family reportedly descended upon her brother's home, frantically searching for the bags of cash he kept there, removing furniture – even pieces that had been rented – and retrieving computer hard drives containing as many as 100 unreleased songs. Their mother, Katherine Jackson, went to court to fight for custody of his three children. The kids had followed Jackson to the hospital in a blue Escalade, and the job of telling them that their father was dead fell to Michael's manager, Frank DiLeo, who had nearly fainted when a nurse broke the news to him. This was the Michael Jackson that the world knew and mocked: the crazy family, the botched plastic surgeries, the two divorces, the charges of child molestation, the financial woes that had left him with debts totaling an estimated $500 million.

But Michael had a different view. In his final days, he not only dreamed of a comeback, he worked as hard as he could to pull it off, maybe as hard as he ever had in his life. He wrote new songs, rehearsed hour after grueling hour to perfect the shows that would pay off his debts and mark his return to greatness, and planned every detail of his comeback – a massive spectacle that had already cost at least $25 million in preproduction alone. Jackson gave the show its title, and the name said it all: This Is It. Jackson knew what people thought of him, and he was going to change their perceptions, just as he had so many times before. High-definition video quickly surfaced of Michael's final rehearsals, demonstrating that the show would have been everything Jackson promised. Columbia Pictures paid the concert promoters $60 million for the rights to create a feature film out of the footage.

In the final months of his life, Jackson thought of nothing but the tour. And those whom he loved and trusted the most were

sure that this was the moment he had been waiting for. "This is real?" asked his friend Deepak Chopra, who spoke with Jackson often in the weeks before his death. "You're coming back for real?"

"For real," said Michael, laughing.

OVER THE LAST 20 YEARS OF HIS LIFE, Michael Jackson slowly lost his grip: financially, artistically and emotionally. It would be comforting to say he merely squandered his gifts, but looking back on his slow-motion deterioration, it seemed like pop music's greatest act of self-destruction.

Jackson's childhood was marked both by massive fame and boundless torment: He often recounted horror stories of the mental and physical abuse he suffered from his father, Joe Jackson. "He practiced us with a belt in his hand," Michael recalled. ("They all got whippin's, but they didn't get no beatings, you know?" Joe Jackson said in his defense.) There were also hints over the years that Michael was a victim of childhood sexual abuse by some unknown party, though he never addressed the issue. Jackson developed an aversion to adult sexuality early on, after being horrified by his brothers' encounters with groupies (sometimes while he was in the room) and his father's casual adultery. Outside of the young boys who accused Jackson of abuse, the only person who has claimed to have had a sexual relationship with him was his first wife, Lisa Marie Presley, who stayed with him for less than two years. Jackson decided that he could literally be Peter Pan – and will himself to remain a child even as he hit middle age.

By the early Nineties, Jackson was starting to be known more for his eccentricities than for his music. It didn't help that he had cultivated that image for a time before the release of 1987's *Bad*, reportedly planting false stories about buying the Elephant Man's bones and sleeping in a hyperbaric chamber. But in 1993, his world exploded when a 13-year-old boy who had spent many nights at Jackson's Neverland Ranch accused Jackson of sexual molestation. As the public learned for the first time that Jackson routinely had sleepovers with young boys, the singer fell deep into a painkiller addiction, cutting short a tour and entering rehab in London. When he returned to the U.S., he was forced to undergo a strip search – authorities wanted to compare his

POWER COUPLE
Jackson with then-wife Lisa Marie Presley at the MTV Music Video Awards in 1994. The pair were married less than two years.

genitals to a description by his accuser. Jackson barely made it through the procedure, at one point hitting his own doctor, according to one report. Within a month, Jackson paid more than $20 million to reach a civil settlement with his accuser's family. The alleged victim refused to testify against Jackson, and prosecutors never brought criminal charges.

True or not, the accusations warped the course of the rest of Jackson's life. "Some people can handle things being said about them, some people can't," says Stevie Wonder, who had known Michael since their Motown days. "When everything is said and done, some of the people were only doing it for the mockery, the self-aggrandizement. If there was pain Michael felt, they were part of it."

By 1995, Jackson was literally falling apart. Under hot, bright lights on the set of the video for "Scream" that year, he was practicing dance moves when his hand brushed his heavily altered nose. The tip of it – actually a prosthesis – flew across the floor, and Jackson began screaming hysterically. Crew members ran after it. "There was a hole, man, a little hole right where the tip of the nose should be, a perfectly circular opening," says a source who was in the room that day. "It was kind of disgusting. I felt bad for the guy."

Another source says that Jackson would sometimes abandon the prosthesis altogether, showing up at meetings with a bandage over the hole. Despite his denials, he also had his skin bleached, though friends say he did it as a means of dealing with vitiligo, a skin disease that causes pigmentation loss and would have left his skin blotchy.

"When Michael proudly showed me the results of his first experiments with bleaching his skin white (his chest looked like he was wearing a pale white vest), I was horrified and told him that the doctor who did this was a criminal and that he should go no further," recalls John Landis, who directed the video for "Thriller." "He did not speak to me for almost two years after that. And when I did see him again, his plastic surgeries had progressed to the grotesque."

Though Jackson would say that he was proud of being black, he took pains to keep his skin looking as pale as possible. At an inaugural concert for Bill Clinton in 1993, Stevie Nicks remembers, one of Jackson's aides asked to borrow some make-up from her. "I was using a light Chanel foundation," she says. "Michael sent back a note to say thanks, but the shade wasn't light enough for him."

Jackson was oblivious to how his appearance came off. When he showed up in 1991 with ghostly-pale skin in the video for "Black or White," he had absolutely no sense that viewers might apply the title to his own life. "Look at the guy's face, and I mean that in a very sad way," says a music-industry source who worked with Jackson. "If he didn't see that, why would he see the irony in that title?"

For one of Jackson's final music videos, 2001's *Guys and Dolls*-in-Cuba-style "You Rock My World," director Paul Hunter hid the star's ravaged features as much as he possibly could – there's even an extended dance sequence where Jackson performs entirely in silhouette. "One of the tricks that we did was we said, 'We're in this gangster world, so let's come in with some swagger, get your hat brim pulled down, get a do-rag going,'" Hunter says. "What I tried to do was not call too much attention to it."

IN MAY 1994, JACKSON married Lisa Marie Presley, who acknowledged to ROLLING STONE nearly a decade later that she had doubts about his relations with children. "Did I ever worry?" she said. "Of course I fucking worried. Yeah. I did. But I could only come up with what he told me. The only two people that were in the room was him and that kid, so how the hell was I going to know? I could only go off what he told me."

Presley, who maintains that her relationship with Jackson was genuine and sexual, nonetheless told ROLLING STONE that she wasn't sure if Jackson loved her: "As much as he can, possibly. I don't know how much he can access love, really. I think as much as he can love somebody, he might have loved me. It was always like a mind that was constantly working. It was a scary thing – somebody who's constantly at work, calculating, manipulating. And he scared me like that."

Presley wasn't Jackson's first choice as spouse – he initially proposed marriage to his friend Brooke Shields, suggesting that they could adopt children together. She sweetly declined. Though he had frequently described his Eighties relationship with Shields as romantic, the relationship was always platonic – the actress had simply given him permission to describe her as a girlfriend. "I told him, 'If you need me to do that for you, I'll be that person,'" Shields says. "'I will take that title, but no one will understand what that means to us.'"

Shields seems uncertain about the nature of Jackson's sexuality. In the Eighties, she says, he was both scared of and curious about sex – Shields was a teenager, and both she and Jackson were virgins at the time, she says. "But as he got older, to me, he just became more asexual," says Shields.

Outside of the world of show business – where he was savvy enough to become the world's biggest singer and make a business move as brilliant as buying the Beatles' publishing catalog – Jackson's self-image was pathologically distorted. "He saw himself as a child; he really, really did," says the music-industry source who worked with him. "It was dangerous. I don't think he had the appropriate boundaries that an adult would have with a child, because he didn't see himself as an adult. Was he having these sleepovers? Absolutely. He didn't deny it; he said there's nothing wrong with him sleeping with boys. In the course of that, might there have been fondling? Probably, I don't know, I wasn't there. But the point is his state of mind was really like a child. He was a peer to these kids. I know that disgusts a lot of people, and I'm not saying that's right or wrong, but I'm saying as a fact, that that really was his state of mind."

"He was a deeply troubled guy, who had a miserable childhood with brutal parents, who was trying to remain a child," says Landis. "His fantasy life and superstardom combined to isolate him from reality and ended up in tragedy. He was a good kid driven mad by circumstance. I will always be fond of him and sad for him."

But Jackson's true self could be as hard to pin down as his facial features – even his high speaking voice was apparently an affectation that came and went. "I was always saying [to Michael], 'People wouldn't think I was so crazy if they saw who the hell you really are: that you sit around and you drink and you curse and you're fucking funny,'" said Presley. "'And you have a bad mouth, and you don't have that high voice all the time. I don't know why you think that works for you, because it doesn't anymore.'"

In an anguished blog entry after Jackson's death, Presley recalled a conversation with Jackson about her father, who died isolated and addicted to drugs. "At some point [Michael] paused," Presley wrote. "He stared at me very intensely, and he stated with an almost calm certainty, 'I am afraid that I am going to end up like him, the way he did.'"

In the wake of the 1993 charges, Jackson's music turned claustrophobic and paranoid, as did his life. He retreated to Neverland. "He didn't want to go out into the outside world, which was so cruel and too much to handle," says Shields. Execs at his record label, Epic, tried to push him to record and released 1997's remix-heavy *Blood on the Dance Floor* as a compromise when they couldn't get a full album out of him.

STRANGE BEDFELLOWS
Jackson with second wife Debbie Rowe, whom he married in 1996. The couple had two kids.

"There was a noticeable change in his behavior," says the music-industry source, adding that most people attributed the change to his addiction. "He'd leave messages at odd times of the night, there was paranoia, some slurred speech. He started spending time in other parts of the world where he was revered, and you would see him always being the guest in some Saudi sheik's palace or in some place in Korea, because he was so huge in other parts of the world, where he could still sell out stadiums." He repeatedly announced plans for theme parks and other ambitious ventures in various countries – none of them happened. He signed a deal to play two turn-of-the-millennium concerts – they never happened either.

By 2000, Jackson was deep in debt, facing multiple lawsuits and reportedly participating in voodoo rituals against his perceived enemies – a lengthy list. And if there was any doubt that Jackson's judgment was severely off, he proved it with a bizarre crusade against his record label, which he blamed for the disappointing sales of his 2001 album *Invincible* (which may have cost as much as $30 million to record). He even paraded around New York with signs proclaiming Tommy Mottola, then-head of Sony Records, to be a racist devil. The attack was so extreme that the Rev. Al Sharpton – who had initially signed on to assist Jackson's crusade – ended up condemning it.

CHILD WELFARE
Jackson dangling his son Prince Michael II, a.k.a. "Blanket," over a hotel balcony in Berlin, 2002.

His career fading, addicted to prescription painkillers and running out of cash, Jackson agreed to cooperate on an all-access documentary with British journalist Martin Bashir, which aired in 2003. He was convinced that a candid look at his life – complete with quotes such as "If there were no children on this earth, I would jump off the balcony immediately" – would make the world finally understand him and help him launch a *Thriller*-level comeback. Just before the documentary's airing, one of Jackson's then-associates, Marc Schaffel, got word of its contents and had the unpleasant job of telling Jackson that Bashir's film was a complete disaster. Jackson – who was during this time taking a mix of OxyContin, Demerol and Xanax ("whatever he could get his hands on," Schaffel says) – was shattered. "He went nuts," Schaffel says. It was the first in a series of tantrums that would culminate in him tearing a room apart in Las Vegas.

Around this time, Jackson went into hiding. Fellow child star Donny Osmond, an old friend, remembers getting a call from Jackson. "I said to him, 'Mike, where are you?'" Osmond recalls. "He said, 'Please don't tell anybody. I rented a touring bus, and I took my kids, and we're somewhere in Arizona.' I said, 'What are you doing?' He said, 'I don't want anyone to see me. I don't want anybody to know where I'm at.'

"I said, 'Mike, do me a favor. Come to Utah. No security. Come to my house. No guards. No nothing. No one will even know you are here. And just come to my backyard, and we'll swim and we'll talk.' And I didn't say this blatantly, but I wanted him to experience what a normal family was like, what a normal atmosphere was like. And he shut down.

He didn't take me up on it. And that's the last time I ever spoke to him."

But Jackson couldn't hide forever. Before long, the boy seen holding Jackson's hand and leaning lovingly on his shoulder in the documentary – a recovered cancer patient – told investigators that Jackson had molested him. The police raided Neverland on November 18th, 2003, confiscating pornography and other evidence, and when Jackson found out, he went "berserko," according to Schaffel. While out on bail, Jackson did another interview, this time with *60 Minutes,* in which he again defended his relationships with young boys. The night it aired, December 28th, 2003, Jackson reportedly took a near-fatal overdose of morphine.

Jackson was ultimately acquitted in a tragicomic criminal trial that featured Jay Leno taking the stand and jurors scoffing at the loopy testimony of the alleged victim's mother, who had gotten a full body wax at Jackson's expense. But the prosecution succeeded in tarnishing what remained of Jackson's image, with lurid though inconclusive testimony of Jackson getting a young boy drunk before molesting him in his bedroom.

As he was driven home in a motorcade on June 13th, 2005, just after his acquittal, the mood in the car was subdued. Arriving at Neverland, Jackson went upstairs and turned to Dick Gregory, a comedian and family friend who had known Michael since he starred in *The Wiz.* Jackson grabbed Gregory and clutched him tightly. "Don't leave me," he begged. "They're trying to kill me."

Gregory had the feeling that Jackson was referring to the whole world. Michael seemed paranoid and dehydrated. "Have you eaten?" Gregory asked him, knowing that Jackson often went without food for days.

"I can't eat," Jackson responded. "They're trying to poison me."

"Do me a favor," Gregory told him. "Get out of here. All of these people have double-crossed you."

Jackson had long lived in an alternate world of yes men who seemed to come and go, many of them bilking the singer or accusing Michael of bilking them. There was Schaffel, the former gay-porn producer who advised Jackson for years, and Al Malnik, a lawyer who reportedly once represented mobster Meyer Lansky. There were two German "entrepreneurs" who managed to get Jackson to endorse a sports cola, known only as "Mystery Drink," which was briefly sold during the *HIStory* tour. And there was his security detail from the Nation of Islam, which was rumored to have come to blows with several of Jackson's brothers who had expressed concern over the Nation's growing sway over Michael's life.

Jackson knew he had to get out – but his choice of a savior only made things weirder. That June, to help him resolve his finances and escape the glare of the media spotlight, Jackson turned to a man he had never met: Sheik Abdullah bin Hamad bin Isa Al-Khalifa, a prince of Bahrain. The sheik had befriended Michael's brother Jermaine, who had converted to Islam and spent four months living in Bahrain. Abdullah helped pay off some $2.2 million in legal fees for Michael, and

UNDER SUSPICION
Left: Michael walks into court clad in pajama pants for his 2005 trial on molestation charges with his father, Joe (right). This page: On the stand after being sued by a promoter for canceling two millennium concerts (above) in 2002; his 2003 mug shot (center); at Santa Barbara County Superior Court (right).

by the end of the month, Jackson – with his three young children and staff in tow – went to live with the prince. There were rumors of private shows for the sheik. Abdullah, who had musical aspirations of his own, later said that he and Michael were working on a record together.

Even then, Jackson was dreaming of a comeback. "A tour was always in the works," says Miko Brando, Marlon's son and a longtime friend and bodyguard of Michael's. "It was just to get himself ready to go back to work and be productive. Michael is too much of a perfectionist just to sit around and not do anything. He was always creating music, creating ideas. He knew how to put things together, what worked, what the public was hungry for."

As always, though, things seemed to go wrong quickly. After Jackson left Bahrain in 2006, Abdullah filed suit against him, claiming that he had spent enormous sums on Jackson – from renting a palatial home to buying him body lotions and a Ferrari – in the expectation that Michael would record an album of songs he had written. Jackson fled to Ireland, where he continued to work on music. But he never released any songs.

Jackson moved to Las Vegas after returning from abroad in 2006, taking up residence with his children in a 10-bedroom mansion west of the Strip. Jack Wishna, a wheeler and dealer in the gaming industry, was trying to help Michael land a series of shows in Vegas that could pay off his mounting debts, but the deal wasn't going well. Wishna would later tell CNN that the singer seemed "drugged up" and "incoherent" and was often so weak that he needed a wheelchair to get around. Jackson and his children rarely left the mansion, except for shopping excursions. When they did go out, the kids wore feather-and-mesh masks, their father by their side in his odd uniforms from some imaginary army, replete with epaulets and armbands. Photographers had captured him as he was pushed around in the baking Las Vegas sun in a wheelchair, wearing a surgical mask and pajamas.

The Vegas shows were eventually canceled because of Jackson's condition, Wishna said. Around that same time, Jackson's sister Janet reportedly tried to stage an intervention with Michael to curb his drug use but failed. In the summer of 2007, Jackson was contacted by AEG, one of the world's leading concert presenters. The company was about to open the O$_2$, an 18,000-seat arena on the banks of the River Thames in eastern London, and it needed someone with the star power to fill it. Randy Phillips, the CEO of AEG Live, was friendly with Jackson from the 1980s, when they had worked together on a deal for the sneaker company LA Gear. Phillips flew to Las Vegas to meet with Jackson and his advisers, and they sat down for dinner in the private wine cellar of a luxury-condo complex.

Jackson arrived in sunglasses and a hat, but he seemed disengaged as Phillips made his pitch for a series of shows at the O$_2$ arena. "He was listening," recalls Phillips. "He wasn't excited." Jackson said he loved the long-running show that Celine Dion had been doing in Vegas, and he was interested in doing something similar. But not long after the meeting, Phillips got a call from Raymone Bain, one of Jackson's advisers at the time, who said the star wasn't ready to perform again, let alone commit to an arduous, ongoing series of concerts.

Then in October 2007, creditors began foreclosure proceedings on Jackson's beloved Neverland. "He didn't think about

FALLING APART
*After various surgeries on his nose, Jackson's face
was ravaged. While filming the video for "Scream,"
in 1995, he accidentally brushed off the prosthesis
on the tip of his nose.*

money – it wasn't his motivator," says Phillips. "Which may have been why he spent so much."

IN 2008, WITH THE VEGAS CONCERTS OFF THE table, Jackson turned to Wall Street to bail him out. Given a spending habit that some said had hit $35 million a year, Jackson had sustained his lavish lifestyle by taking out a reported $270 million in loans from Bank of America, much of it secured by his Neverland Ranch and his stake in the Sony/ATV publishing catalog, which includes the music of the Beatles and the Jonas Brothers. But Bank of America had sold the loan package to Fortress Investments, a New York firm that specializes in distressed debt.

In March 2008, Jackson announced that he had made a deal with Fortress – which at one point was reportedly charging him 20 percent interest on his old loans – to stop the firm's foreclosure proceedings on Neverland, his 2,700-acre ranch with a zoo, a movie theater, two railroads and an amusement park with a Ferris wheel, go-karts, bumper cars and cotton-candy stands. He bought the place in 1988 and admitted it was his way of claiming the childhood he never had. "I'm just putting behind the gates everything I never got to do as a kid," said Jackson. But soon after the 2005 child-molestation trial, Jackson would leave Neverland forever.

The deal to stave off foreclosure never materialized. Instead, Michael took the advice of someone he had just met: Tohme Tohme, a Lebanese financier from Los Angeles. According to Tohme, he was contacted in 2008 by Michael's brother Jermaine, who asked if he could help save Neverland. The two flew to Las Vegas and met with Michael, who put his trust in Tohme. The financier quickly persuaded his friend Tom Barrack, the billionaire CEO of Colony Capital, to meet with Jackson. Barrack, whose investment fund owns the Las Vegas Hilton and dozens of other resorts and casinos, prides himself on his "cautious contrarianism," which he defines as "investing in out-of-favor sectors or markets to exploit capital or product misalignments." If ever a sector was out of favor or misaligned, it was Michael Jackson – and Barrack had the resources to rescue him from Fortress.

In May 2008, Colony and Jackson formed a holding company to own the property jointly, halting Neverland's foreclosure. They reverted to calling it by its pre-Jackson name, Sycamore Valley Ranch, and immediately started renovation work, most likely with an eye toward selling it. Three years after Jackson's departure from Neverland, the ranch was empty, silent and "in shambles," according to a court declaration filed by Darren Julien, founder of Julien's Auctions, which had been hired to sell off pieces of the property. "Buildings, amusement rides, industrial equipment, personal automobiles and Jackson's personal zoo and Tipi village were falling apart," he said.

Julien spent months working with the Jackson camp, carefully cataloging the immense contents of the ranch. "It was like Disneyland collides with the Louvre," says Julien. "Only in Neverland could you see an 18th-century statue next to a monumental castle next to a statue of butlers and maids." But in spring 2009, the auction came to an abrupt halt when one of Jackson's own companies filed suit against Julien's, claiming it had not consented to the sale. The sudden reversal underscored what many in Jackson's world had long known: that Jackson was surrounded by competing advisers, and that who was in or out of favor seemed to change on a whim.

If Jackson wasn't going to sell off his stuff from Neverland, he would have to find another way to raise money. In fall 2008, Barrack sat down with Phillips and described Colony's plans for restructuring the mess that was Jackson's finances. In November, Jackson flew to Los Angeles from his home in Vegas and met with Phillips at the Bel-Air Hotel. Once again, they spoke about the possibility of a comeback – but this time, Michael seemed keenly interested.

As he and Phillips spoke for hours, Jackson opened up about everything he wanted. He talked about making movies that he would star in and direct. He had already spent millions on one: *Ghosts,* a short, family-friendly horror film starring himself and based on a screenplay he had commissioned from Stephen King. He wanted to make another album. And he wanted to tour. But more than anything, Phillips recalls, Jackson wanted to be able to show his kids what he did, what made people on the street mob him when he left the house.

"He wanted people to see his work and not just talk about his lifestyle," says Phillips. "Michael was a very smart marketing person. People say he was feeble and manipulated, but he was powerful and a manipulator. He was ready. He wanted to clean up his finances." Jackson told the promoter that he wanted to pay off his debts so he could buy a house in Las Vegas that he had fallen in love with, one that belonged to the Sultan of Brunei. It would be his new Neverland. "He was ready to stop living like a vagabond and settle down and earn money again," says Phillips. "He wasn't stupid – he knew there wasn't a fairy godmother coming. The house and making movies were huge to him."

After the meeting, Phillips debriefed the owner of AEG, Phil Anschutz. "I believe Michael needs to do this financially," Phillips told his boss. "And he's ready to do this emotionally. He's ready to get back on the horse." Jackson agreed to kick off a worldwide comeback tour with 31 performances at the O$_2$ arena, beginning on July 8th, 2009. According to Phillips, the number of shows wasn't arbitrary – Jackson chose it so he would have 10 more shows than Prince, who had opened the arena with a series of spectacular concerts in 2007. Michael, it seems, had been engaged in his own private competition with Prince since 1987, when Prince refused to perform a duet with him on "Bad." Two decades later, Jackson was still eager to upstage his rival and remind the world who was King.

ONE DAY NEAR THE END OF FEBRUARY, Kenny Ortega answered the phone in his home office in Sherman Oaks, California, and heard a soft, familiar falsetto on the other end of the line. "Kenny," the caller said, "it's Michael." Right away, Ortega heard something in Jackson's voice that had been missing for a long time: excitement. The two had become friends in the early 1990s, when Ortega choreographed Michael's *Dangerous* tour, and they worked together again on the *HIStory* tour. Following his child-molestation trial in 2005, Jackson had largely dropped out of touch with his friends in the music business. But now, as Jackson described the comeback tour he was putting together, Ortega heard a focus in the star that had been absent for years. Michael sounded sharp and clear as he told Ortega that he wanted this to be the most spectacular show in music history. "This is it," Jackson said, echoing what would eventually become the show's title.

Jackson would make a number of calls to old friends and associates whom he had let go or fired over the years. "It was the old team," says Ortega. Frank DiLeo, who had been pushed out of Jackson's inner circle two decades earlier, was brought back as manager, along with choreographer Travis Payne and long-time lawyer John Branca, who had helped Jackson buy his stake in the Sony/ATV catalog and the rights to all his masters. "He understood that he would be working toward financial freedom, and he was very excited about that," says DiLeo. "It encouraged him – he knew he was working toward something."

For AEG, booking Jackson for a series of concerts at the O$_2$ arena was a huge gamble. The insurance costs alone were monumental, and everyone knew that Jackson did nothing on the cheap. As part of the deal, AEG set up a million-dollar development fund for creating a movie version of "Thriller," which Michael was eager to produce. But despite the costs, the potential upside was huge: What if AEG could do the impossible and bring Michael Jackson back to the world? "People told me I was crazy, that I would get my heart broken by him," says Phillips. "But I just believed in him. How many times in your career do you get to touch greatness? I thought it was worth the risk."

In March, within hours of Jackson telling a screaming mass of fans in London that he was preparing for what he called his "final curtain call," more than 1.6 million people signed up to buy tickets. Given the numbers, Phillips called Tohme and asked if the pop star might consider adding more shows to the schedule. How could they limit themselves to 31, Phillips asked, when there was so much money waiting to be made?

Jackson called back 20 minutes later and told Phillips he would do 50 shows – as long as AEG did two things for him. First, he wanted to be provided with an English country estate with rolling hills, greenery and horses for the kids. Second, he wanted a ceremony held at the end of the tour to commemorate some as-yet-to-be-defined accomplishment by Jackson for the *Guinness Book of World Records.* It was the two seemingly contradictory things that he had striven for his entire life: to live in seclusion, surrounded by children and animals, and to be recognized as the greatest performer in history.

JACKSON FLEES USA
*In Dubai with race-car champion Mohammed bin
Sulayem (right) and Sheik Abdullah bin Hamad bin
Isa Al-Khalifa, son of Bahrain's king. Left: With an
unidentified child in Bahrain, 2006.*

The 50 O_2 shows sold out in only three days. Jackson was delighted: Maybe the comeback he always dreamed of was finally around the corner. "Isn't it great?" Jackson said to Will.i.am of the Black Eyed Peas. "Isn't it amazing? A million tickets!"

By that point, Jackson had moved his family to Los Angeles, renting a seven-bedroom château in the Holmby Hills from Mexican-textile magnate Hubert Guez, who had recently taken over as CEO of luxury T-shirt maker Ed Hardy. After signing a lease for $100,000 a month (the house had been on the market for $38 million), Jackson settled into a routine of sorts, going out mainly at night. But it didn't take long before the fans and paparazzi tracked him down and set up vigil outside his new home. Every day a dozen or so people waited outside, some who had come from as far away as Switzerland and Sweden just to catch a glimpse of Jackson, even if it was only a hand waved through the window of one of his two blue Escalades. Some of them would tail Jackson to Beverly Hills, where he regularly visited his longtime dermatologist, Dr. Arnold Klein.

Klein's office is where, in the mid-1980s, Jackson met Debbie Rowe, his second wife and the mother of his two oldest children, Prince and Paris. Klein, who declined to comment for this story, has said that he was treating Jackson for vitiligo and working to help rebuild his damaged nose. Klein has insisted that he did not overmedicate Jackson, saying he sedated the singer only during painful medical procedures.

Some days when Jackson left Klein's office, he seemed drowsy and out of it. "It's not a good day for him," his security guards would tell the assembled well-wishers. "He's tired." But some longtime fans weren't buying it. "Sometimes the guards would say that he just went to the doctor and he's on medication," says one die-hard fan. The fan says Jackson visited Klein the Monday before he died, when Michael's security detail brought him to the dermatologist's office at 9 a.m. – an early-morning mission seemingly scheduled to avoid detection by fans and paparazzi.

According to one source, Jackson also had a rampant eBay addiction, staying up late at night to make purchases on one of the numerous accounts he maintained. He also went on secretive shopping expeditions in L.A., taking his kids to the Ed Hardy store in West Hollywood to check out the clothing maker's wares, or to an antique shop he loved called Off the Wall. Sometimes he would just take the kids out with his security detail and drive. Despite being a purported health nut, he would sometimes stop for Kentucky Fried Chicken along the way.

But for the first time in years, Jackson had a show to focus on. In March, auditions for the comeback tour began at Center-Staging, one of the primary rehearsal spaces in Los Angeles. From the start, Michael took a hands-on role in the shaping of the show, urging those around him to conduct a sort of intergalactic talent search. "Think about the greatest artists and dancers in the world," he told Ortega. "Let's find them."

STRANGE DAYS
*Leaving a hotel in Beverly Hills with children Prince and
Paris in 2003. Jackson often masked his children in
public in order to keep photographers from taking
pictures of their faces.*

More than 5,000 dancers applied, and Ortega and his team narrowed it down to 700. Jackson was at the final auditions in Hollywood, sitting next to Ortega, fully focused. "Let's get closer," he told the choreographer. "I want to see their eyes." When he spotted a promising dancer, he'd say, "That one there, the girl on the end – she's so beautiful."

At the end of March, just three months before the first concert was scheduled to kick off, a crew of dozens of musicians and dancers and technicians began showing up for daily rehearsals at CenterStaging – putting in long hours, seven days a week. In the beginning, Jackson would show up only a few times a week, sitting with Ortega for several hours and going through his huge archive of material – old photographs, videos, records. They were hoping to capture that essence, that special something that made him the King of Pop.

Jackson was determined to give the fans everything they wanted. He ordered a website set up so fans could vote for which songs he would perform, and he and Ortega used it to begin compiling a 30-song session list. Jackson, who had a lifelong interest in magic, seemed eager to blow people's minds.

"When the show opens, I don't want to hold anything back," he told Ortega. "I want this to be the most spectacular opening the audience has ever seen. They have to ask themselves, 'How are they going to top that?' I don't even care if they're applauding. I want their jaws on the ground. I want them to not be able to sleep, because they are so amped up from what they saw."

To get in shape for the grueling tour, Jackson started working out a few times a week with Lou Ferrigno, star of the TV show *The Incredible Hulk*. The two had met years earlier at a party, when Ferrigno noticed Jackson staring at him from across the room, recognizing him as the Hulk. "He was like a kid," says Ferrigno, who would arrive in the morning to be greeted by Jackson's children racing around the house, playing games.

Jackson was painfully thin – although pushing six feet, he weighed only 127 pounds – and he'd suffered several injuries over the years. He and Ferrigno would go to a back room that was equipped with a treadmill. Jackson didn't want to build muscle, so they worked out gently, stretching with a rubber band and an exercise ball. Jackson wore black tuxedo pants, a black T-shirt, black shoes and black socks while he worked out, so he wouldn't have to change when he went to rehearsals afterward. "He was a hoot," says Ferrigno. "Many years ago he told me he was extremely lonely. But when I was with him he looked very fulfilled and happy. He was like Mr. Mom."

Jackson clearly loved being at home with his children, and he often engaged in his own childlike antics. "He was a jokester," says Ferrigno. "He'd call my phone, sometimes disguising his voice for 10 minutes. I was thinking I had a stalker. He would say his name was Omar and that he was looking for me."

But "Omar" did more than play pranks on his friends. According to TMZ, Jackson also used the name to fill prescriptions for the cornucopia of painkillers and sedatives he was taking. In

2007, a Beverly Hills pharmacy called Mickey Fine filed a complaint against Jackson for not paying his bill for prescriptions – a total of $101,926.66, dating back to 2005. Court documents from the investigation into child-molestation charges against Jackson included interviews with two former Neverland staffers who reported that Jackson regularly took as many as 40 Xanax a night in order to sleep.

ALTHOUGH JACKSON WAS PLAYING A CENTRAL role in shaping the comeback tour, taking the stage to prepare was another matter entirely. While the crew logged long hours at Center-Staging, Jackson preferred to work from home most days. Those around him were getting nervous. According to Phillips, AEG's initial budget of $12 million for preproduction had more than doubled. But when the promoter pressed Jackson on the $150,000 a month he had agreed to pay his physician, Conrad Murray, Michael rebuffed him sternly. "Look," Jackson said, "my body is the mechanism that fuels this entire business. Like President Obama, I need my own personal physician attending to me 24/7."

Others began to press Jackson to rehearse more. "I had my concerns if he was ready, and I questioned him," says Ortega. "There were days when I was like, 'Are you going to show up? Are you really going to be here? You need to do this.'" Citing the need for more setup time in London, Ortega asked for the opening show to be pushed back five days, to July 13th.

Many close to Jackson are convinced he never could have mustered the physical and mental stamina to make it through all 50 shows. "I believe he was going to do the first show, and it would have been good – one of the incentives he had was that his kids had never actually seen him perform," Schaffel says. "Maybe two weeks later, he would have done another show, but that would have been it."

In early June, Dr. Murray mediated a meeting at Michael's home between Jackson and Ortega, who felt the star needed to come to rehearsals more often. Jackson listened quietly to the tour director, but he didn't seem alarmed. "I know my schedule," he said calmly. "Just trust me."

But after that, Jackson started coming to rehearsals all day, every day. To those around him, he seemed focused and attentive to every detail. "I like to refer to Michael as a gamer," says DiLeo. "He's the quarterback. He's the star of the team, and in practice, quarterbacks are easygoing. But game day, he's turning it on."

"He was rusty in the beginning, sure, he'd miss some notes," says the show's musical director, Michael Bearden. "But he would always say, 'That's why we rehearse.' And the last two or three rehearsals, he was ready to do that show. He knew it, he had that glow, that swagger about him. MJ is the master closer. He's got amazing muscle memory. When he gets in front of his fans up on that stage, it's just magic."

At rehearsals, Jackson quickly took charge. Orianthi Panagaris, a guitarist who performed with Carrie Underwood at this year's Grammys, recalls coming in for an audition and being told to play "Beat It." Jackson sat in front of her on a couch. "I was so nervous," she says. "From the couch he told me to crank up my solo. He was clapping at the end, he was really happy. He came over to me and grabbed my arm, and started walking me up and down the front of the stage area. He said, 'When you're playing the solo, I want you to chase me!'"

Some around Jackson were concerned about his heavy reliance on prescription drugs. "I became aware of it in 2005," says Deepak Chopra. "I brought it up with him many times. His assistant would call frequently about it, saying he was being given medication by a lot of doctors. He would go to great lengths to get it – if one doctor didn't give it to him, he'd try another. It was an addiction that was created and perpetuated by doctors."

For the most part, nights seemed to be the biggest problem for Jackson – he had complained of insomnia for years. But it was also the time when he felt a higher power was channeling creativity to him. "I didn't get a whole lot of sleep last night," he would tell Ortega. "I was up working on music. That's when the information is coming, and when it's coming you gotta work."

"Michael," Ortega joked with him, "why can't you make a pact with your higher power so that you could put these ideas on the shelf until after July 13th?"

"No," Jackson said. "Then he might give them to Prince."

Despite his workouts with Ferrigno, Jackson remained thin, almost emaciated. "I was concerned about his weight," says Phillips. "When I started with him, he was a little heavier – heavy for him might have been 130 pounds. He was like the absent-minded professor – he would get so engaged in the creation of the show that he'd forget to eat. To the point where Kenny Ortega used to cut up his chicken breast and feed him broccoli, like a kid, as they worked. I actually brought an associate of mine to just remind him to eat, stuff like that."

Part of Michael's inspiration for the tour was his concern about global warming. Three weeks before his death, Jackson sent Chopra a CD, hand-delivered to his home in Carlsbad, California. "The music is a very soft, mellow piece," says Chopra. "It's called 'Breathe.' He wanted to do a song about the environment, and he wanted me to help him with the lyrics. There were big ideas behind the lyrics – how the trees are our lungs, the Earth is our body."

Indeed, Jackson's worldview seemed to have incubated and grown during his time off the stage. During rehearsals, he often talked about what was going on in the world. "He'd built up a big arsenal of things he wanted to communicate," says Ortega, who found Jackson to be surprisingly engaged in politics and the environment. "He felt time was running out, and he really wanted to dig in and participate. He'd say, 'Do you know this about the rainforest?' or 'Let's bring in Norman Lear and Deepak. Who else do you know?'"

Sometimes those ideas were expensive. Those who worked on the show say they never saw any sign of the financial pressure Jackson was under. Indeed, he seemed to enjoy spending money as much as ever. Ortega recalls he often had to keep Jackson's dreams in check. "You want us to go to Victoria Falls and shoot the waterfall from a helicopter?" he'd say to Jackson, who wanted the video for the show's closing number. "Do you know how much that costs?" But Jackson didn't seem to care. "Money was not his motivating factor," says Phillips. "It was just doing something greater than anyone else had ever done before. That's what motivated him."

O N THE LAST NIGHT OF HIS LIFE, JACKSON arrived at the Staples Center for six hours of a full run-through. First he had a meeting with Phillips, AEG president Tim Leiweke, his manager DiLeo and Grammy producer Ken Ehrlich. They were going over ideas for a Halloween special they were putting together: the network debut of *Ghosts,* Jackson's short film, which would incorporate clips of a live performance of "Thriller" from London. Afterward, Jackson went into another room and spent about an hour going over the 3-D effects for the show. He ate dinner, chicken breast and broccoli. Then he went to his dressing room and came out for three hours of performance.

The closer was slated as "Earth Song," from *HIStory,* one of Jackson's favorites. An impassioned ballad about the state of the world, it ended with a repeated refrain asking about the victims of humanity's rampant and heedless development, from crying whales to ravaged forests. "What about death again?" Jackson sang at the ballad's conclusion. "Do we give a damn?"

A KING IN EXILE
Michael at his Neverland Ranch in 1993. Shortly after his trial, he left the property forever, living in Bahrain and Ireland.

Those who witnessed the performance – seasoned professionals who had worked with the best in the business – were awestruck. Standing before them was the Michael they all remembered, the artist who had grown from a child singer to forge a whole new style of pop. When Jackson walked off the stage, he hugged DiLeo. "This is our time again," he told his manager. "It's time for us to take it back."

The rehearsal was over, but no one wanted to break the spell by leaving. "He was bioluminescent," recalls Ortega. "When he finished, we all stayed there, just messing around." Michael was ready. In only 19 more days, he would take the stage in London, and the world would know, once again, that the King of Pop was back.

Ehrlich, who has produced the Grammy Awards for three decades, sat in the audience, awed: "I turned to somebody and said, 'This is amazing!' For so many years I have watched Chris Brown and Justin Timberlake and Usher and the Backstreet Boys and En Vogue all imitate Michael Jackson – and now here we were this many years later, and he was going to do it again. I got chills, literally. The hairs on the back of my neck were raised. Those are the moments you hope for."

Finally, as the performers started to drift away, Phillips walked Jackson to his car. Michael put his arm around the promoter. "Thank you for getting me this far," he told Phillips in that whisper of a voice. "I can take it from here. I know I can do this."

THE ESSE

MOMEN

By Rob Sheffield

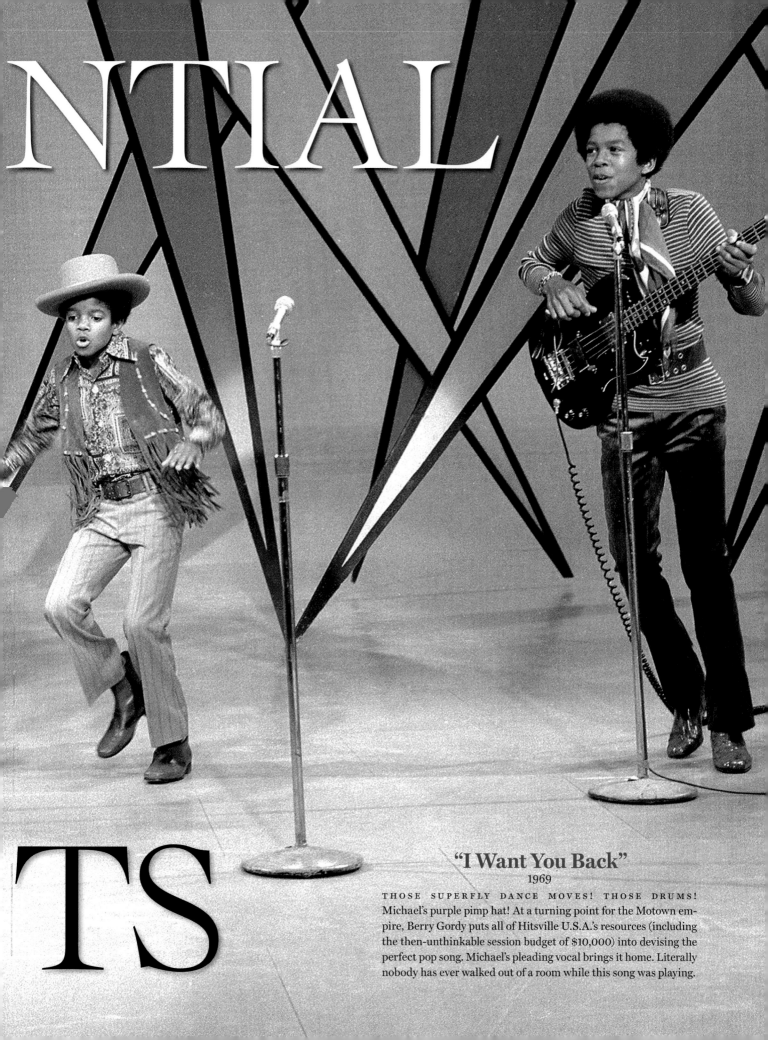

NTIAL

TS

"I Want You Back"
1969

THOSE SUPERFLY DANCE MOVES! THOSE DRUMS! Michael's purple pimp hat! At a turning point for the Motown empire, Berry Gordy puts all of Hitsville U.S.A.'s resources (including the then-unthinkable session budget of $10,000) into devising the perfect pop song. Michael's pleading vocal brings it home. Literally nobody has ever walked out of a room while this song was playing.

DRAWN AGAIN
*From 1984 to 1985, after "Thriller" hit
big, ABC rebroadcast "The Jackson 5ive"
on Saturday mornings.*

"I'll Be There"
1970

WITH THIS BALLAD, THE JACKSON 5 BECAME THE FIRST act ever to hit Number One with their first four major-label singles. They could no longer be dismissed as any kind of kiddie novelty – all the brothers float their voices back and forth, pledging a fantasy of eternal devotion. This song has been covered countless times (Mariah Carey took it back to Number One), but nobody has ever topped the way Michael threw himself into the line "Let me fill your heart with joy and laughter."

"Got to Be There"
1971

HIS FIRST SOLO SINGLE, AND A FIRST TASTE OF THE MATURE, introspective Michael to come, it sold more than a million and a half copies after coming out in the fall of 1971. The song itself is hardly childhood stuff ("Got to be there in the morning"?), with bittersweet minor-key harmonies that should have been beyond the reach of a young thing. Yet Michael coasts over the jazzy chords and lush orchestration, handling each key change like a born soulman. He'd just turned 13.

The Jackson 5ive
1971-73

FOR COUNTLESS SEVENTIES KIDS, THIS SATURDAY-MORNING cartoon (with "ABC" as the theme song) was the first experience of the J5's timeless soundtrack of playground funk, like a mix of Sly and the Family Stone with Fat Albert's Junkyard Band. It was more psychedelic than *Scooby-Doo*, with a better beat than *Hong Kong Phooey*, so good that ABC resurrected it for Saturday mornings in 1984, after *Thriller* hit big. Michael admitted later he watched it all the time, saying to himself, "I'm a cartoon!"

"Dancing Machine"
1974

THE BROTHERS WERE GETTING TOO OLD FOR TEENY-BOPPER appeal, chafing at the artistic limitations of the Motown hit machine, where not even Michael was allowed to contribute to the songwriting or production. But their last major Motown hit (and early disco experiment) was a taste of beats to come. While MJ was quietly watching the pros work the studio, he was soaking up the tricks ("like a hawk," as he admitted) he'd use to conquer the world.

"Rock With You"
1979

BELIEVE IT OR NOT, THERE WAS A
time when using the word "rock" in a disco
tune was scandalous. That's why you can't
call *Off the Wall* crossover – Michael was
disco and proud, but Michael's mirror-ball
glimmer was so seductive that the whole
music world just crossed over to him.
Nobody could resist the finale, where he
stretched the word "girl" into a six-syllable
psalm. His androgyny was irresistible: He
was the girliest boy in the world, yet the
most lavished with girl love, and he wasn't
the least bit embarrassed about it.

FRIGHT NIGHT
Jackson on the set of the
"Thriller" music video,
in 1983. Directed by
John Landis, the clip
ran 14 minutes.

"Shake Your Body (Down to the Ground)"
1979

DANCING HIS WAY OUT OF THE CONSTRICTIONS OF MOTOWN, seizing his first shot at creative control, MJ leads his brothers to the promised land. The lyrics introduce his spiritual yearning ("I need to do just something to get closer to your soul"), while the groove really does shake your body down to the ground. Goodbye, yellow-brick road; hello, future of pop.

"Don't Stop 'Til You Get Enough"
1979

MAKE A LIST OF THE TOP 10 "OOOOH!" SCREAMS IN HISTORY, and this hit has at least six of them. MJ introduces the world to his grown bad self, rocking harder than anything on rock radio, yet sleek and debonair enough to make the rest of the Top 40 sound like hot air. Who else could get away with that murmured spoken-word introduction? Who else could wear white socks with a tux and still look so cool?

"Heartbreak Hotel"
1980

AN R&B SMASH FOR THE JACKSONS, THIS WAS TOO DARK for the radio – it peaked at Number 22 on the pop charts – but huge in the clubs. Michael swore it wasn't an intentional Elvis reference, though the record company got nervous and gave it the moronic new title "This Place Hotel." (That's one of the few moments in his career for which nobody has *ever* claimed the credit.) But Elvis would have appreciated how it mixes up old-time religion, a taste of sex and a lot of fear.

"Billie Jean"
1983

SIX MINUTES OF COSMIC FUNK DEMENTIA, AN INSTANT Number One despite being one of the strangest and most disturbingly personal songs ever to grace the radio. Quincy Jones tried to talk Jackson out of putting it on the album, but party people still quake to the bass line of Louis "Thunder Thumbs" Johnson. The song ended up putting a sticking point between Michael and Quincy – Michael felt he deserved a co-producing credit, since the demo version he presented to Jones sounded almost exactly like the version on *Thriller*. Quincy disagreed.

"Beat It" Video
1983

THIS WAS THE SONG THAT WAS SUPPOSED TO MAKE Michael acceptable to discophobes, but "Billie Jean" had already done that, so it became a victory lap instead. For the video, he swoops into a ghetto garage full of gangbangers and saves the day like a teen angel, while Eddie Van Halen's guitar solo keeps him running with the devil.

Motown 25 Special
1983

EVERYBODY HAD ALREADY SEEN THE MAN MOVE TO "Billie Jean," but on May 16th, 1983, 50 million fans tuned in hoping he'd break out something new. He did, gliding with superhuman grace. Lots of dancers have claimed they're the one who taught Michael to moonwalk – Shalamar's Jeffrey Daniel had just done it on the U.K.'s *Top of the Pops* – but Michael undoubtedly made it his own. Fred Astaire called him the next day to say, "You put them on their asses last night."

"Human Nature"
1983

IN A WAY, THIS WAS AN APOLOGY FOR "THE GIRL IS MINE," his doggone ridiculous Paul McCartney duet – a delicate ballad on the surface, but heart-wrenchingly emotional soul, finessed brilliantly by the guys from Toto. Michael never sounded warmer, braver, breathier, more emotionally vibrant. This deserved to hit Number One, but you know what did instead? "Say Say Say," an even more ridiculous McCartney duet.

"Thriller" Video
1983

THIS 14-MINUTE JOHN LANDIS MOVIE WAS NEVER REALLY much of a music video – the dialogue was funny, but you sure couldn't dance to it. It showcases Michael's beautiful smile but hints at the darkness in his soul as he dances in front of a chorus line of zombies.

"State of Shock"
1984

THE LAST GREAT MOMENT FOR THE JACKSONS AND a redemptive bit of sleaze on their otherwise dead-on-arrival *Victory*. It's just Michael with Mick Jagger, two old pros trading goofball sex shtick over a funky faux-Stones guitar groove, milking it about two minutes too long but somehow turning that into part of the joke.

"We Are the World"
1985

MICHAEL'S ORIGINAL DEMO VERSION WAS A QUIET BALLAD with a melancholic touch; it became the star-studded USA for Africa extravaganza that immortalized Bob Dylan's golden pipes, Dan Aykroyd's dork glasses and Lionel Richie's upraised thumb. It also marked the final appearance of the gentle young Michael of the *Thriller* moment, singing the line Prince didn't show up for ("When you're down and out, and there seems no hope at all") more convincingly than Prince could have.

Captain EO
1986

IN BETWEEN "THRILLER" AND "BAD," JACKSON ARRIVED at Disney's Tomorrowland, a couple of years too late to fit in. This 17-minute 3-D film started showing at the Disney theme parks in 1986, a sci-fi fairy tale made with Francis Ford Coppola and George Lucas with the theme song "We Are Here to Change the World." Disneyland stopped showing *Captain EO* in 1997, for perhaps obvious reasons.

"Bad"
1987

EVERYONE WONDERED IF MICHAEL COULD STILL CAPTURE people's attention, but this song, the second single from the album of the same name, proved that he had the knack, especially with an opening line like "Your butt is mine." Naturally, it went straight to Number One. Post-*Captain EO* Michael was a completely different personality, a grim and weary adult feeling burdened by the world. His youthful glow was a thing of the past; he wasn't having any fun, and he wanted us all to know that.

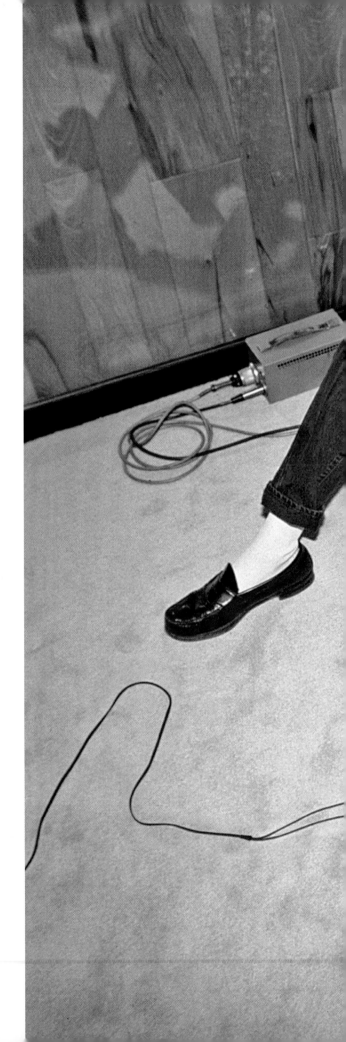

I'LL BE YOUR MIRROR
*Michael and a gospel choir
singing "Man in the Mirror"
at the 1988 Grammys.*

"Man in the Mirror" at the Grammy Awards
1988

WHEN PEOPLE FIRST HEARD THE STUDIO VERSION, HE sounded full of himself. But at the Grammys, onstage at Radio City Music Hall in New York, Jackson took the song to church, with a full-blown gospel production that stands as one of his most stunning vocal workouts. Michael didn't win a single award that evening, but in a way, this was as majestic and definitive as the *Motown 25* moonwalk.

Moonwalker
1989

IN CASE ANYBODY OUT THERE HADN'T NOTICED THAT Michael had an issue or two, this bizarro film – Jackson had hoped for a theatrical release, but instead it went straight to video in the U.S. – rammed it home with cartoons, Claymation and *Transformers*-style sci-fi violence. Who else could inspire a video game where you get to kill people with your dancing prowess?

"Black or White"
1991

AFTER A FEW YEARS AWAY, MICHAEL CAME BACK STRONG with this first single off *Dangerous*, as if the worst was behind him and there was all the time in the world for him to keep creating effervescent pop hits like this one. He could grab your heart with a line like "I believe in miracles/And a miracle has happened tonight," but he could also grab your body with those hyperactive guitar stutters and herky-jerky funk beats.

"In the Closet"
1992

HIS EARLY-NINETIES WORK IS THE ONLY TIME MJ really capitulated to music trends, hopping the new jack swing beats of Teddy Riley, yet he sounded right in the pocket. With a mysterious female spoken-word vocal (Was that Madonna? Princess Stephanie? La Toya?) and a Naomi Campbell video, this is a one-of-a-kind item in his songbook.

The Grammy Awards
1993

ACCEPTING A LIFETIME-ACHIEVEMENT AWARD FROM sister Janet, MJ gave the world the last thing anyone expected: a moment of genuine human emotion. His hug with Janet coaxed tears out of anyone who'd ever cared about him. He looked lucid, spontaneous, even playful. ("Me and Janet *are* two different people!" – hey, this guy is funny? Who knew?) He seemed to realize how much people loved him, and it was cathartic to see him able to reciprocate. It was a final display of his charm, right before the whole act came crashing down.

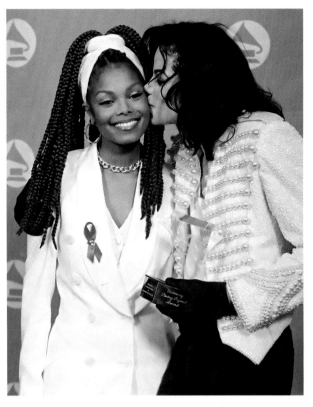

SISTER ACT
Michael kisses Janet in thanks for giving him his Grammy Legend award.

Blood on the Dance Floor
1997

HIS LAST ANGRY GASP AND A TRUE ODDITY: AN ALBUM by Michael Jackson that barely anybody heard. A barrage of quasi-industrial remixes and freakouts, disconnected from any concept of pop music as it existed outside his skull, this was never a hit, although it did end up being the biggest-selling remix album of all time, for whatever that's worth. But it exposes the paranoid rage driving Jackson's music at the end. It was only after Michael's death that people began to notice "Morphine," an ode to Demerol addiction.

"You Rock My World"
2001

HIS LAST CHOICE OF AN OLD-HOLLYWOOD PLAYMATE was Marlon Brando, which made it harder to ignore that Michael had turned into Colonel Kurtz at the end of *Apocalypse Now*. He bid his audience one last farewell with a 30th-anniversary special – scheduled, in a bit of bad luck that guaranteed no one would remember it, the weekend before 9/11 – and made his last visit to the Top 10 with one of the least-memorable things he'd ever recorded. There would be other headlines after this, but here is where the music ended.

TRIBUTES

Jackson's friends, fans and fellow artists celebrate the man and the music

Quincy Jones

The producer worked with Jackson on his three biggest albums

Michael was a master at making every song sound like it completely belonged to him – from "Human Nature," with all the different, kaleidoscopic parts, to "Billie Jean," with three chord changes, almost like a mantra. If you break down "Baby Be Mine," it's like John Coltrane, just disguised with pop lyrics and a pop arrangement. Michael was the most professional artist I ever worked with in my life, the most focused and the quickest to get to the core of a song. He was the best dancer, the best singer; he was a dramatist like Frank Sinatra – he could make you believe anything on a record.

I met him when he was about 12, but when he was about 20, we were working on *The Wiz*, and he said, "Could you help me find a producer for my first solo album?" And I said, "We can't talk about that now, you don't even have a song in *The Wiz* yet!" But I was watching him on the set with Diana Ross singing "Ease on Down the Road," and he was so focused, so disciplined. He didn't miss a thing. I hadn't seen that side of him before. So I said, "How about if I produce the album?" Epic said, "No way, Quincy is too jazzy, he's the wrong guy." But I understood the power of being misunderstood a long time ago. We made the biggest-selling album by a black artist in history up to that time, and they all changed their minds real quick.

Stevie Wonder

One of Michael's mentors since the early days of Motown

I first heard about Michael when he and his brothers were coming to Motown – and then I heard that voice. You couldn't help but be instantly moved by the way Michael sang a song like "I Want You Back" or "I'll Be There" or, later, "The Way You Make Me Feel," which is one of my favorites. One time, Michael and I were riding in an elevator together, and I was singing "The Way You Make Me Feel" to him, and we started going back and forth trading lines, and I told him how much I loved that part where he sang, "Go on, girl," and Michael told me that he took it from my song "Go Home," which made me feel pretty good.

I remember we were on a kind of safari together once in a truck with bars to protect you from the lions. I could hear Michael telling the driver, "Can we get a little closer?" Then I heard a big roar, and suddenly Michael got real quiet.

Smokey Robinson

The Motown legend wrote "Who's Lovin' You" for the Jackson 5

I spent a great deal of time with Michael when he was 10 or 11. A Motown artist named Bobby Taylor and I would take Michael to the golf course just to ride around on the cart while we played. If I hit a bad shot, he'd just laugh and tell me how I should've hit it. He never caddied or took a single swing in his life – he just came along and critiqued.

Donny Osmond

Childhood rivals in the early 1970s, he and Michael remained friends in the decades to come

The Osmonds and the Jackson 5 had hit records at the same time. We were once playing a big show in Canada. The ironic thing is we were both teen idols, and all we wanted to do was go back to the hotel, and – while Joe and Katherine were talking to my father and mother – we went to the other room and played with toys.

I remember a few years ago, I went to Stevie Wonder to play him a cover I had recorded of his song "I Wish." And Stevie said, "Please, please, get close to Mike, because he really needs a

EXIT

MICHAEL'S MENTOR
As a teen, Jackson was influenced by Stevie Wonder's music, watching him in the studio as he recorded 1974's "Fulfillingness' First Finale."

friend right now." So right after that, I went off to Mike's house, and I played the track for him. This is right before everything hit the fan with all the trials. And I said, "We have always been linked in a parallel universe, with us and our families, but we've never actually done anything together." And his face lit up and he said, "What are you thinking?" And I played him "I Wish." And he loved the track with these two kids who are now adults talking about "I wish those days would come back once more." And he said, "I love it, let's do it." We were going to do a duet, and then he called me up as soon as the trial hit and said, "I've got to pull out."

Lionel Richie
A friend since the 1970s, he wrote "We Are the World" with Michael

The first single on *Thriller* was "The Girl Is Mine," with Paul McCartney; I was a huge fan of Paul McCartney. And Michael knew this. I was working in the same studio where they were recording the song at one or two in the morning, and he called and said, "Lionel, come on over." I thought he wanted me to hear a track, and I go into the studio, and Paul McCartney was there. Needless to say, I ended my session for the night. I think Quincy went home that night because we were talking so much. Paul and Michael had so much in common in terms of the fame, and Michael was such a sponge. He asked every question. I think Paul had a blacked-out Suburban, and by the time Paul left, Michael had one too.

The irony of it is that Paul McCartney, Quincy Jones and myself had friends before we were 21. We all had to fight on the playground before we were 21. We all had a girl leave us before we were 21. We went through regular-guy growing-up experiences. But when it came to Michael, you couldn't get to "regular." From seven or eight years old, this brother was singing. I remember him coming right home from tutoring and going right to the studio. They wouldn't have playground time. Jackie and Jermaine had a little bit more of a real experience because they were older. But that door closed early for Michael.

With his whole being, he only wanted to be the biggest and the best there was. But in the later years, it wasn't the playground singing "Wacko Jacko" – it was the whole world saying it. How do you get over that? It tears you down. And the result is, we saw a major artist crumble right in front of our very eyes.

LA Reid
Jackson invited Reid, now chairman of Island Def Jam, to write songs for 1991's 'Dangerous'

Michael was very sweet, but he was a huge competitor. He invited me and my partner, Babyface, to the Neverland Ranch in 1991. He was working on *Dangerous* and asked us to write for the album. We took a helicopter to his house, and it was a very bumpy ride. I must have had a look of terror on my face, and Michael started laughing at me and told me I was soft.

SUPERSTAR JAM
Jones, Richie and Jackson recording "We Are the World" – which Jackson and Richie wrote to raise funds for famine relief in Africa – in Los Angeles, 1985

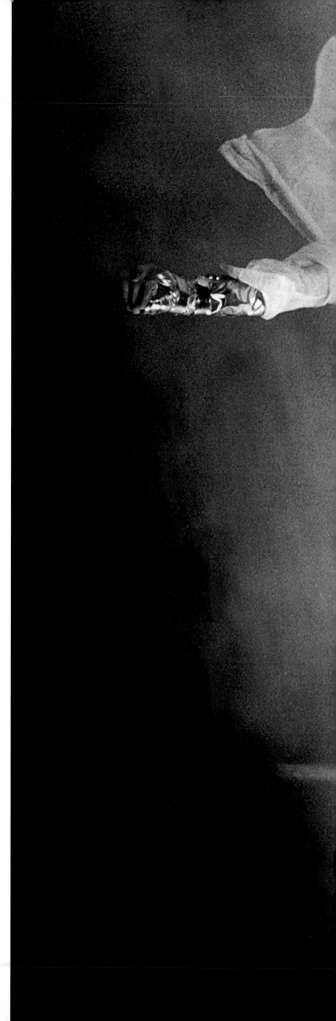

Akon

The singer spent time at Jackson's house, working
on material for a planned comeback album

Mike and I met a couple of years ago through a friend. We
recorded at his home studio, and his kids were always there.
He was always monitoring them – making sure they were doing
their homework, eating right. He would personally cook for
them, always healthy stuff. They were the main focus of his life
– we could be in the middle of recording, and he'd drop everything to make sure they were good.

Martin Scorsese

The Oscar winner directed Jackson in the video for
"Bad," set in a Brooklyn subway station

When we made the "Bad" video, he was open to everything.
Like that scene in the hallway when Wesley Snipes says, "Are
you down, or what?" We did that maybe 40 times. Wesley is a
formidable presence, but Michael stood up to him. The main
thing that struck me was the extraordinary power of his almost
shamanistic persona. I was mesmerized by his dancing. In the
first shot, when his face is looking up toward the camera, there
was a sense of loneliness and victimization. Those images had
a resonance to them.

Across the street from where we shot a scene in Harlem, the
buildings were torn down or condemned. He took me aside: "Do
people live here?" He was overwhelmed by what he saw. In an
apartment on the ground floor of the building where we were
shooting, there was an unfortunate person in bed, coughing
and on his last days. Michael said, "Do you see what's in there?"
I said, "Yeah, I know." But even the guy who was sick in bed
knew who Michael was.

Slash

The Guns n' Roses guitarist played on 'Dangerous' and
appeared on the 1992 tour with Jackson

One of the cool things about Michael is he just let me do my
thing. We were doing a show in Italy, and Jennifer Batten, his
guitar player, wanted me to follow these choreographed moves
that she was doing. And I wouldn't have it – there was no way.
We were in the dressing room and she's complaining and runs
to Michael. It was the first time I'd seen him get shrewd and
serious and bossy; he told her to fucking just leave Slash alone.

I would just get up and do my thing, but every so often I
would look up and be dazzled by how naturally and how fluidly
he worked. Michael lived in the entertainment business, that's
the only life he's known ever since he was a little kid, and there
was a sense of detachment from reality with him. He was completely in tune when he was doing anything having to do with
music, but he seemed completely detached when it involved
anything else. He was genuinely great to witness in person. He
could have 80 people onstage all doing the same dance move in
unison, but he was the one guy who had that natural flow that
nobody could match.

CHARITY ROCKS
Jackson and Slash at a Jackson-organized benefit concert for Kosovo's children in Munich, Germany, 1999.

**PRETTY
YOUNG THINGS**
*Crow – then a backup
singer – with Jackson on
the "Bad" tour in 1988*

Ne-Yo

*Jackson recruited the singer to submit tracks
for his planned comeback album*

About two years ago Michael called my cellphone, and I hung up on him, because I thought somebody was playing. Michael Jackson don't call your damn cellphone. A couple of minutes later, he called back, and I was like, "Oh, damn." I lied and told him I was going through a tunnel and we got disconnected. He wanted to meet somewhere secluded, so we met at Lyor Cohen's house because they're good friends. I don't get star-struck, because people are people, but Michael was an energy. I felt his presence when I walked into the room. We talked about working together, where he wanted to go musically. I'd submit three or four songs a couple of times a month, and he'd tell me what he liked or didn't like: "Take this part and change it; make the hook stronger." He was being very selective – this was either going to be his comeback album or a very sad attempt, and he didn't want the latter.

Sheryl Crow

*She launched her career as a backup singer
on Jackson's 1987 'Bad' world tour*

I met Michael at the rehearsals for the *Bad* tour in 1987, when I was hired as a backup singer. I was surprised by how shy he was. We were rehearsing the duet "I Just Can't Stop Loving You," and we had a funny joke between us – we were doing a love song and pretending to be very shy about it, and we'd giggle when we touched each other. To see that youthfulness out of somebody who's the most important entertainer in the world was surprising.

Our first three weeks on the road, we played Tokyo in front of 75,000 people. Michael broke into "Human Nature," and he did the sideways moonwalk. I remember standing by the side of the stage thinking, "I'll never see this kind of talent again in my life." I don't care what kind of music you're into – there's something special in him that isn't of this world.

"Weird Al" Yankovic

*The Grammy-Award-winning parody act
credits his career to Jackson*

The first time I pursued Michael Jackson about a song parody, it was a shot in the dark. We're talking about the most popular and famous person in the universe, and here I was, this goofy comedy songwriter. He not only returned our phone calls but he approved it. He thought it was a funny idea. Then when we did the second parody, "Fat," he let us use his subway set for the video, so he's always been very supportive.

The first time I met him in person was when I ran into him at one of his concerts in 1988, when *Even Worse* came out with my second parody, "Fat." I went backstage, and he was seeing a lot of people, but I brought along a gold record of *Even Worse* to present to him, and he was very gracious and thanked me for it and said some nice things. After the fact, I thought, "That's probably the last thing Michael Jackson needs, another gold record for his storage locker." Seeing him in person was otherworldly. He was and continues to be so iconic, it's hard to even conceive of him as a human being.

Our second meeting was a TV-show taping, I think. He was performing "Black or White," and I talked to Michael briefly afterward. He told me he would play my movie, *UHF*, for his friends at Neverland Ranch, and he was very soft-spoken, very quiet, but always very friendly to me.

I considered parodying "Black or White" around that time. but Michael wasn't into it, because he thought "Black or White" was more of a message song, and he didn't feel as comfortable with a parody of that one, which I completely understood. In a way, he did me a huge favor, because I was already getting pegged as the guy who did Michael Jackson parodies, and I decided to go with Nirvana, which wound up revitalizing my career. I don't know what kind of career I would have today if it hadn't been for Michael Jackson. In a very real sense, he jump-started my career. "Eat It" basically changed me from an unknown into a guy that got recognized at Burger King.

Brooke Shields

*In the late 1970s, she and Michael became very close –
two famous teenagers not quite in love*

I was 13 when I first met Michael Jackson. We instantly became friends. Nothing was jaded about him. I just was so impressed by his sweetness. He was thoughtful, sensitive, sweet, and had a funny sense of humor. If you got to talk to him about music or about the future of technology, his voice would get deeper, he would start talking, and it was as if he was this genius.

There were times when he would ask me to marry him, and I would say, "You have me for the rest of your life, you don't need to marry me, I'm going to go on and do my own life and have my own marriage and my own kids, and you'll always have me." I think it made him relax. He didn't want to lose things that meant something to him.

As he grew older and the more he started to change physically, the more asexual he became to me. It was easy for him to be a friend to me, because I was the most celebrated virgin ever; it's ridiculous, but I was America's virgin. You saw women who were more sexual, who wanted to throw themselves at him and feel like they were going to teach him; we just found each other, and we didn't have to deal with our sexuality. As I grew up and started having boyfriends, I would share with him, and he was like a little kid who talked about the bases – what first base was, what second base was, and it sounded very odd to the outside, I can imagine, but to the inside, to someone who's never really left his bubble, you can understand how he would be curious.

The last time I saw him in person was at Elizabeth Taylor's wedding, in 1991. He seemed like his own funny self. We snuck in and took pictures of ourselves next to her dress. We always seemed to revert to being little kids. It was a sanctuary for him, because he knew I never wanted anything from him but his happiness.

40 YEARS OF HITS

A complete guide to Michael Jackson's singles, including his 60 Top 40 hits. Seventeen of them – counting both solo tunes and Jacksons jams – went all the way to Number One

1968   CHART PEAK

The Jackson 5
"Big Boy"
The J5's debut single, released on the Gary, Indiana, label Steeltown in January 1968, sold more than 10,000 copies. The song was rereleased after the master tapes were rediscovered in 1994.

The Jackson 5
"We Don't Have to Be Over 21 (To Fall in Love)"

1969

The Jackson 5
"I Want You Back"   1
The first of four straight Number Ones, this tune was originally written for Gladys Knight.

1970

The Jackson 5
"ABC"   1

The Jackson 5
"The Love You Save"   1

The Jackson 5
"I'll Be There"   1

The Jackson 5
"Santa Claus Is Comin' to Town"

1971   CHART PEAK

The Jackson 5
"Mama's Pearl"   2

The Jackson 5
"Never Can Say Goodbye"   2

The Jackson 5
"Maybe Tomorrow"   20

Michael Jackson
"Got to Be There"   4

The Jackson 5
"Sugar Daddy"   10

1972

Michael Jackson
"Rockin' Robin"   2

The Jackson 5
"Little Bitty Pretty One"   13

Michael Jackson
"I Wanna Be Where You Are"   16

The Jackson 5
"Lookin' Through the Windows"   16

The Jackson 5
"Doctor My Eyes"

Michael Jackson
"Ain't No Sunshine"

Michael Jackson
"Ben"   1
Jackson's first solo Number One was the title track from a horror movie about a boy who befriends a rat. Donny Osmond had been the studio's first pick to record the song, but he was too busy on tour.

The Jackson 5
"Corner of the Sky"   18

1973   CHART PEAK

The Jackson 5
"Hallelujah Day"   28

The Jackson 5
"Get It Together"   28

Michael Jackson
"With a Child's Heart"   50

The Jackson 5
"Skywriter"

1974

The Jackson 5
"Dancing Machine"   2

After a two-year slump, the brothers returned to the Top 10 with this early disco track that introduced America to the Robot.

The Jackson 5
"The Boogie Man"

Michael Jackson
"Music and Me"

The Jackson 5
"Whatever You Got, I Want"   38

The Jackson 5
"The Life of the Party"

1975   CHART PEAK

The Jackson 5
"I Am Love (Parts I & II)"   15

Michael Jackson
"Just a Little Bit of You"   23

Michael Jackson
"We're Almost There"   54

The Jackson 5
"Forever Came Today"   60

The Jackson 5
"All I Do Is Think of You"

1976

The Jacksons
"Enjoy Yourself"   6

1977

The Jacksons
"Show You the Way to Go"   28

The Jacksons
"Goin' Places"   52

1978

The Jacksons
"Find Me a Girl"

The Jacksons
"Even Though You're Gone"

The Jacksons
"Music's Taking Over"

Michael Jackson and Diana Ross
"Ease On Down the Road"   41

The Jacksons
"Blame It on the Boogie"   54

1979 — CHART PEAK

The Jacksons
"Destiny"

Michael Jackson
"You Can't Win (Part 1)" — **81**

The Jacksons
"Shake Your Body
(Down to the Ground)" — **7**
This ultra-funky jam, written by Michael and Randy, was the template for *Off the Wall*.

Michael Jackson
"Don't Stop 'Til You Get Enough" — **1**

Michael Jackson
"Rock With You" — **1**

1980

Michael Jackson
"Off the Wall" — **10**

Michael Jackson
"She's Out of My Life" — **10**

The Jacksons
"Lovely One" — **12**

The Jacksons
"Heartbreak Hotel" — **22**

1981

The Jacksons
"Can You Feel It" — **77**

The Jacksons
"Walk Right Now" — **73**

The Jacksons
"Time Waits for No One"

The Jacksons
"The Things I Do for You"

Michael Jackson
"One Day in Your Life" — **55**

1982

Michael Jackson and Paul McCartney
"The Girl Is Mine" — **2**

Jackson and McCartney cut two hits together: "Say Say Say," for McCartney's *Pipes of Peace*, and this one, for *Thriller*. In 1985, Jackson outbid McCartney for the Beatles' catalog.

1983 — CHART PEAK

Michael Jackson
"Billie Jean" — **1**

Michael Jackson
"Beat It" — **1**

Michael Jackson
"Wanna Be Startin' Somethin'" — **5**

Michael Jackson
"Happy"

Michael Jackson
"Human Nature" — **7**
Keyboardist Steve Porcaro of Toto wrote this song with help from Carpenters' lyricist John Bettis.

Michael Jackson
"P.Y.T. (Pretty Young Thing)" — **10**

Paul McCartney and Michael Jackson
"Say Say Say" — **1**

1984

Michael Jackson
"Thriller" — **4**

Michael Jackson
"Farewell My Summer Love" — **38**

The Jacksons
"State of Shock" — **3**

Michael Jackson
"Girl You're So Together"

The Jacksons
"Torture" — **17**
After *Thriller*'s success, Michael had to be coaxed into this reunion. This song also features Jermaine's first appearance since 1975.

1987

Michael Jackson
"I Just Can't Stop Loving You" — **1**

Michael Jackson
"Bad" — **1**

Michael Jackson
"The Way You Make Me Feel" — **1**

1988

Michael Jackson
"Man in the Mirror" — **1**

Michael Jackson
"Dirty Diana" — **1**

Stevie Wonder and Michael Jackson
"Get It" — **80**

Michael Jackson
"Another Part of Me" — **11**

Michael Jackson
"Smooth Criminal" — **7**

1989 — CHART PEAK

Michael Jackson
"Leave Me Alone"

Michael Jackson
"Liberian Girl"

The Jacksons
"2300 Jackson Street"

1991

Michael Jackson
"Black or White" — **1**
Sheryl Crow collaborator Bill Bottrell helped transform this *Bad* leftover into Jackson's first Number One hit of the 1990s.

1992

Michael Jackson
"Remember the Time" — **3**

Michael Jackson
"In the Closet" — **6**

Michael Jackson
"Jam" — **26**

Michael Jackson
"Heal the World" — **27**

1993

Michael Jackson
"Give In to Me"

Michael Jackson
"Who Is It" — **14**

Michael Jackson
"Will You Be There" — **7**
The eighth single from *Dangerous* flew up the charts after appearing in *Free Willy*.

Michael Jackson
"Gone Too Soon"
The ninth and final single from *Dangerous* was Michael's tribute to AIDS victim (and friend) Ryan White. Usher sang it at Jackson's memorial service.

1995

Michael Jackson and Janet Jackson
"Scream" — **5**

Michael Jackson
"You Are Not Alone" — **1**
Jackson's 17th and final Number One hit, from his *HIStory* album, was penned by R. Kelly. The video features Jackson caressing a top-less Lisa Marie Presley.

Michael Jackson
"Earth Song"

1996 — CHART PEAK

Michael Jackson
"This Time Around"

Michael Jackson
"They Don't Care About Us" — **30**

1997

Michael Jackson
"Blood on the Dance Floor" — **42**
Jackson didn't deem this track worthy of a spot on *Dangerous*, but six years later it became the first single from his *Blood on the Dance Floor* collection. It was his first lead-off single to not hit the Top Five since he left Motown in the 1970s.

Michael Jackson
"Stranger in Moscow" — **91**

Michael Jackson
"HIStory"/"Ghosts"

2001

Michael Jackson
"You Rock My World" — **10**

Michael Jackson — **14**
"Butterflies"
Jackson's last Top 40 hit, written by Floetry's Marsha Ambrosius, was the second single from his ill-fated final album, *Invincible*. Jackson, who believed Sony didn't promote the disc aggressively enough, protested outside the label's office in 2002.

Michael Jackson
"Cry"

2002

Michael Jackson
"Heaven Can Wait"

2003

Michael Jackson
"One More Chance" — **83**

The last single released during Jackson's lifetime was written for his compilation album *Number Ones*. The ballad hit stores the same day that police officers raided Neverland Ranch, beginning the sexual-assault case against the singer.

CONTRIBUTORS

Anthony DeCurtis

Anthony DeCurtis is a contributing editor at ROLLING STONE. He won a Grammy for his liner notes to the Eric Clapton box set *Crossroads*.

Jon Dolan

Jon Dolan is a frequent contributor to ROLLING STONE.

Ben Fong-Torres

Ben Fong-Torres became an editor at ROLLING STONE in 1969. He is working on a book about Quincy Jones.

Mikal Gilmore

Mikal Gilmore is a longtime contributing editor at ROLLING STONE and the author of several books, including *Stories Done*, about the cultural icons of the Sixties and Seventies.

Brian Hiatt

Brian Hiatt is an associate editor at ROLLING STONE.

Gerri Hirshey

Gerri Hirshey is the author of *Nowhere to Run: The Story of Soul Music* and *We Gotta Get Out of This Place: The True, Tough Story of Women in Rock*.

Claire Hoffman

Claire Hoffman is a contributing editor at ROLLING STONE and an assistant professor of journalism at the University of California, Riverside.

Alan Light

Alan Light is a former senior writer for ROLLING STONE and a frequent contributor to *The New York Times*.

David Ritz

David Ritz is the author of *Divided Soul: The Life of Marvin Gaye* and the co-author of memoirs by Ray Charles, Etta James and Aretha Franklin.

Rob Sheffield

Rob Sheffield is a contributing editor at ROLLING STONE and the author of the memoir *Love Is a Mix Tape: Life and Loss, One Song at a Time*.

Touré

Touré is a contributing editor at ROLLING STONE and the author of the novel *Soul City* and the short-story collection *The Portable Promised Land*.

Douglas Wolk

Douglas Wolk is a critic and the author of *Reading Comics: How Graphic Novels Work and What They Mean*.

With reporting by David Browne, Andy Greene, Austin Scaggs, Evan Serpick and David Wild